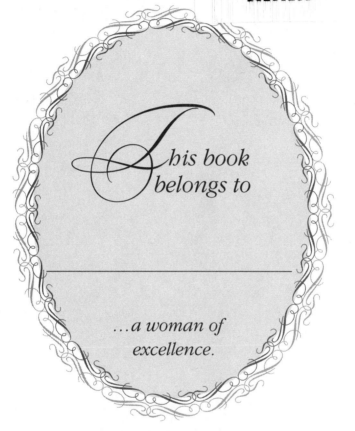

*his book
belongs to

...*a woman of
excellence.*

Discovering the Treasures of a Godly Woman

Elizabeth George

HARVEST HOUSE™ PUBLISHERS

EUGENE, OREGON

Unless otherwise indicated, all Scripture quotations are taken from the New King James Version. Copyright ©1982 by Thomas Nelson, Inc. Used by permission. All rights reserved.

Verses marked KJV are taken from the King James Version of the Bible.

WOMAN AFTER GOD'S OWN HEART is a series trademark of The Hawkins Children's LLC. Harvest House Publishers, Inc., is the exclusive licensee of the federally registered trademark WOMAN AFTER GOD'S OWN HEART.

Cover design by Terry Dugan Design, Minneapolis, Minnesota

Acknowledgments

As always, thank you to my dear husband, Jim George, M.Div., Th.M., for your able assistance, guidance, suggestions, and loving encouragement on this project.

DISCOVERING THE TREASURES OF A GODLY WOMAN

Contents

Foreword

For some time I have been looking for Bible studies that I could use each day that would increase my knowledge of God's Word. In my search, I found myself struggling between two extremes: Bible studies that required little time but also had little substance, or studies that were in-depth and demanded more time than I could give. I discovered that I wasn't alone—there were many other women like me who were busy yet desired to spend quality time studying God's Word.

That's why I became excited when Elizabeth George shared her desire to create a series of women's Bible studies that offered in-depth lessons that could be completed in just 15-20 minutes per day. When she completed the first study—on Philippians—I was eager to try it out. I had already studied Philippians many times, but this was the first time I had come to understand exactly how the whole book fit together and how it can truly be lived out in my life. Each lesson was simple but insightful—and was written especially to apply to me as a woman!

In the Woman After God's Own Heart® Bible study series, Elizabeth takes you step by step through the Scriptures, sharing wisdom she has gleaned from more than 20 years as a women's Bible teacher. The lessons are rich and meaningful because they're rooted in God's Word and have been lived out in Elizabeth's life. Her thoughtful and personable guidance makes you feel as though you are studying right alongside her—as if she is personally mentoring you in the greatest aspiration you could ever pursue: to become a woman after God's own heart.

If you're looking for Bible studies that can help you grow stronger in your knowledge of God's Word even in the most demanding of schedules, I know you'll find this series to be a welcome companion in your daily walk with God.

—LaRae Weikert
Editorial Managing Director,
Harvest House Publishers

efore *You* *Begin*

In my book *A Woman After God's Own Heart*®, I describe such a woman as one who ensures that God is first in her heart and the Ultimate Priority of her life. Then I share that one crucial way this desire can become reality is by nurturing a heart that abides in God's Word. To do so means that you and I must develop a root system anchored deep in God's Word.

Before you launch into this Bible study, take a moment to think about these aspects of a root system produced by the regular, faithful study of God's Word:

- *Roots are unseen*—You'll want to set aside time in solitude— "underground" if you will—to immerse yourself in God's Word and grow in Him.

- *Roots are for taking in*—Alone and with your Bible in hand, you'll want to take in and feed upon the truths of the Word of God and ensure your spiritual growth.

- *Roots are for storage*—As you form the habit of looking into God's Word, you'll find a vast, deep reservoir of divine hope and strength forming for the rough times.

- *Roots are for support*—Do you want to stand strong in the Lord? To stand firm against the pressures of life? The routine care of your roots through exposure to God's Word will cultivate you into a remarkable woman of endurance.[1]

I'm glad you've chosen this study out of my A Woman After God's Own Heart® Bible study series. My prayer for you is that the truths you find in God's Word through this study will further transform your life into the image of His dear Son and empower you to be the woman you seek to be: a woman after God's own heart.

In His love,

Elizabeth George

Lesson 1

A Godly Woman

Proverbs

*P*oetry has been a fascination of mine since my early days in junior high school. Maybe it's because my mother was an English teacher, and not just an English teacher, but a *Shakespearean* English teacher! Therefore I was continually exposed to Elizabethan language and poetry.

Are you perhaps wondering, *What does poetry have to do with the book of Proverbs in the Bible and with the Proverbs 31 woman?* That's a great question. For, you see, the book of Proverbs is a form of poetry in the Hebrew language. But unlike English poetry with its rhyme and meter, Hebrew poetry uses what is called *parallelism.* As you'll soon see, each proverb, or saying, usually has two lines, each with a parallel relationship to the other.

Discovering the Treasure...

In each lesson, this section in our Bible study is dedicated to looking at the Bible, to observing what the Scriptures say about the topics and Bible passages addressed. But before we approach Proverbs 31:10-31, I want us to learn a few things about the book of Proverbs and about Hebrew poetry.

1. *The book of Proverbs*—This marvelous book of the Bible is *treasure!* It's a treasure-house filled to overflowing with wisdom—God's wisdom. It's even categorized as one of the wisdom books of the Bible. Within its 31 chapters are many references to wisdom's being like treasure. Note how these proverbs refer to wisdom and allow these descriptions to whet your appetite for discovering the treasure of the Proverbs 31 woman. Also note any suggestions as to *how* we are to discover the treasure.

   —Proverbs 2:4

   —Proverbs 3:13-14

   —Proverbs 8:10-11

2. *The style of the proverbs*—To communicate wisdom through poetry, the book of Proverbs generally uses three types of parallelism, or line structure, to create a poetic

effect. As you learn about parallelism, look in your Bible at the verses indicated and make notes regarding the wisdom found there.

—*Synonymous parallelism*—Here the meaning in the first line is paralleled by a similar meaning in the second line.

—Proverbs 1:2

—Proverbs 31:20

—*Antithetical parallelism*—Here the first line is the opposite of or contrasted with the second line, which usually begins with the word "but."

—Proverbs 10:1

—Proverbs 31:30

—*Synthetic parallelism*—Here the second line simply continues the thought of the first line with the second line usually starting with "and."

—Proverbs 3:6

—Proverbs 31:13

3. *A few exceptions*—As with most language guidelines, Proverbs has its exceptions. Not all verses have two lines. Some verses, called triplets, have three lines. For instance, what happens to those who hate knowledge and scorn wisdom in Proverbs 1:27?

Now describe the actions of the worthless person in Proverbs 6:13.

And note the early morning activities of the Proverbs 31 woman in Proverbs 31:15.

Developing Godly Excellence...

I'm glad you took the time to understand more about the structure of the poetry we'll be studying throughout this Bible study. And now it's time for you to revel in the exquisite poetry of Proverbs 31:10-31. Beloved, this poetry cannot be excelled. Why? Because God wrote it! "All Scripture is given by inspiration of God" (2 Timothy 3:16). It is God-breathed. It comes from God. So let's listen as God Himself speaks to us through His glowing poetic description of a truly godly woman, His woman of excellence.

- *The woman*—Read Proverbs 31:10-31 now. This passage comprises the text of this Bible study. And I invite you to take your time as you read. Linger over each verse of this unmatched poetry. And as you make your way through it, pay attention to the many instances of imagery used to describe this outstanding lady. Also consider what a treasure this godly woman is. In fact, she is a woman God chooses to praise (verse 30), and each verse contains a jewel, a shining gem of her character. Check here when done. _____

- *Her character*—List ten of her character qualities. (Be sure to note the verses that point to each quality.)

_____   _____

_____   _____

_____   _____

_____   _____

_____   _____

- *Your character*—As you study, don't get discouraged as God unveils this treasured woman and her many virtues through these 22 verses! Our job is to desire the treasure and discover the treasure. And we'll do it one verse at a time, one jewel at a time.

Look again at the ten qualities you listed. Then choose one that may be lacking in your life or perhaps needs a little extra attention. Which one is it, and what do you plan to do to give it greater prominence in your daily life?

A Heart in Pursuit of Excellence

My friend, I want you to know that I'm working these exercises right along with you. Indeed, I've been working my way *through* the life of this godly woman in Proverbs 31 for 30 years now as I continue to seek to work her godly virtues *into* my life! I hope and pray that this is your heart's desire too. Indeed, she's been called "The Noble Woman"[2] and "The Virtuous Woman."[3]

The Proverbs 31 woman is truly a woman of excellence who models for us the godly traits that God highly esteems and exalts. Regardless of your background or how you were raised, this woman is yours. God has preserved His portrait of her in your Bible. She's yours to look at, to admire, to inspect, to study, to emulate, and to point others to. And she'll always be there for you to pore over, to visit with, to draw upon, and to be refreshed by. Truly, hers was a heart of excellence, and in this study of her many qualities, I pray that you will desire to pursue her excellence. As Proverbs 31:29 says of her,

> *Many daughters have done well,*
> *But you excel them all.*

esson 2

An Alphabet of Godliness

any years ago, it was my joy to teach children in a small preschool. One thing that marks little ones between three and five years old is their excitement about learning. It was especially fulfilling (and fun!) to help them learn their alphabet. My team teacher and I used word pictures, rhymes, and anything else that would help these tots build a good foundation upon which to learn to read.

As we begin this study of Proverbs 31:10-31, we must first notice *who* the teacher is, and *who* the student is who is receiving this dazzling, concise, and brief description of a woman of godly excellence. And we want to pay particular attention to the style of the teaching—*how* the teacher taught.

Discovering the Treasure...

Begin by reading Proverbs 31:1-9 in your personal Bible. Check here when done _____.

1. *A pupil*—Most scholars agree that Proverbs 31:1-9 reflects a mother's instructions to her young son. According to these verses, what was the son's name?

   List at least five lessons or five cautions this young leader-in-the-making was taught by his godly mother.

   _____

   _____

   _____

   _____

   _____

2. *An alphabet*—Perhaps to help the reader learn this information, the author organized the description of an excellent wife into an alphabetic acrostic. Each of the 22 verses (10-31) starts with a consecutive letter in the

Hebrew language's 22-letter alphabet. This approach is not unique to this passage of Scripture only. Look at several other passages using this same alphabetical approach. Jot down anything that catches your eye or attention or speaks to your heart in each.

—Psalm 25

—Psalm 34

—Psalm 119

—Lamentations 1-4 (Hint—Divide chapter 3 by 22, the number of letters in the Hebrew alphabet!)

Developing Godly Excellence...

- *A teacher*—As we begin our study of Proverbs 31, we meet what many believe to be the woman behind the picture of this ideal woman, the mother of King Lemuel. She must have exhibited many of the qualities she is about to describe. How else could she teach so intelligently about them? And now, turning from her to you, are there any areas of your life that you need to work on before you can instruct others in those same areas?

- *A mandate*—What also stands out about the mother of King Lemuel is that she saw the teaching of her son about life, leadership, and marriage as a mandate, as one of her responsibilities. Do you see yourself as a teacher of good things (Titus 2:3)? Whom has God brought into your life that you can—and should—teach? Are you faithfully teaching your own precious children (Proverbs 1:8 and 6:20)? Why or why not?

A Heart in Pursuit of Excellence

Life is a cycle of being taught and then teaching, of being mentored and then modeling. Don't fail to take every opportunity to pursue godliness and to learn from older, wiser women. And don't fail to take every opportunity to teach others, beginning with your own children, about God's standards for life and godly living.

And, my fellow student of God's Word, don't fail to allow the woman of Proverbs 31 to teach *you* the excellent qualities God desires in His women! Let her godliness model for you and mold your heart and life into one of virtue, strength, and beauty.

Won't you bow your head now and offer thanksgiving to God for His godly woman? She is indeed one of His beautiful gifts to you, a treasure! She is here in Proverbs 31 to inspire, instruct, and encourage you when you fail, when you find your vision dimming, or when you sense your priorities shifting. A fresh visit with the woman who is beautiful in God's eyes will renew your vision, restore your strength, and rekindle your love for God and your commitment to His magnificent plan for your life!

A Godly Woman Is...Priceless

Proverbs 31:10

*O*nce read about a woman who took the youth group from her church to view the fine art treasures at a famous art museum. Determined that they would see it all, she whisked her group from room to room, from painting to painting, from display to display. However, each time she criss-crossed the museum on the run, she caught sight of one particular room where a gentleman was seated on a bench across from one painting. He remained on that bench for the entire time, drinking in the glory of one masterpiece.

Dear one, as we step into this study of the woman God puts on display in Proverbs 31:10-31, purpose to do like the man above did. Purpose to pay attention to detail, to appreciate the fine art of His trophy of gracious beauty, and to seek to comprehend God's message to your heart. Ask God to give you understanding, to reveal to your heart the depth of the treasure of true womanly excellence. Then, as in everything, beseech His able help in reaching toward the excellence revealed in this splendid and priceless woman.

Now, let's discover her first outstanding quality.

Discovering the Treasure....

Begin by reading Proverbs 31:10-31 in your personal Bible. Check here when done _____. Then write out verse 10.

1. *An army*—As we seek to describe the wonderful woman in Proverbs 31, realize that the word "virtuous" or "excellent" is used some 200-plus times in the Bible to describe an army of men, men of war, and men prepared for war. This Old Testament word refers to *a force* and is used to mean "able, capable, mighty, strong, valiant, powerful, efficient, wealthy," and "worthy."[4] Its primary meaning involves military strength. According to the few references below, what kinds of men were considered virtuous?

   —Exodus 18:25   —Ruth 2:1

   —Joshua 1:14   —1 Samuel 9:1

   —Joshua 6:2-3   —1 Chronicles 12:25

Just as the two forces of mental toughness and physical energy are primary traits of an army, they also mark God's Proverbs 31 woman.

2. *A woman*—The root word for "virtuous" or "excellent" is used only four times in the Bible to describe a woman or women. Look at them now.

Ruth 3:11—What did the man Boaz say about Ruth?

What do you learn about Ruth's character in Ruth 1:16-18 and 2:11?

And about her physical condition in Ruth 2:2,17,23?

Proverbs 12:4—How is this excellent woman described, and what does this imply about her?

And how is the other kind of woman described, and what does this imply about her?

Proverbs 31:10—How is this excellent woman described, and what does this imply about her?

Proverbs 31:29—What accolade does the husband of the Proverbs 31 woman have for his wife?

3. *A question*—Now, back to Proverbs 31:10. What is the question asked regarding this woman?

4. *A priceless treasure*—What is said about the woman in Proverbs 31:10 that indicates her value? What words strike you most and why?

(As a point of information, different translations of Proverbs 31:10 use different words to describe what a treasure this woman is. Some use "rubies." Some use "coral." And some use "pearls." Whatever the translation—and whatever the jewel—each was considered to be a priceless treasure.)

5. *A rarity*—The choice of descriptive words used to describe God's ideal woman ("who can find?" and "far above rubies") indicates that she's a rarity. She must be searched for and sought after because she is so rare, just as rubies, coral, and pearls are also rare and hard-won treasures. Nevertheless, what does God's Word say in the verses that follow about the man who goes to the trouble to find and marry a virtuous woman?

—Proverbs 12:4

—Proverbs 18:22

—Proverbs 19:14

Developing Godly Excellence...

This section of our study is devoted to responding to what we are discovering from God's Word about each quality that makes up the fiber of the Proverbs 31 woman. It's a time to think through what you're learning about godly character and about being a godly woman. Review your discoveries about each of the topics above and then answer the questions.

• *A woman of excellence*—How do you measure up in mental toughness and physical energy, and what improvements must be made?

Which one of the references to the four "excellent" and "virtuous" women spoke most to your heart and why?

• *A priceless gem*—After learning what "virtuous" and "excellent" mean, why do you think such a woman is so rare?

Have those who know you found a virtuous, noble, excellent woman? Please explain your answer.

A Heart in Pursuit of Excellence

I still remember the day I discovered the meaning of the word "virtuous" or "excellent." It was a red-letter day that became a turning point in my growth as a Christian woman.

As a result of the conviction of the Holy Spirit through what I was reading in the Bible and of a simmering desire for the priceless character and strength of this godly woman, I decided to pursue her excellence. And my first step was making some willful changes in the Work Department. I began to apply my strength and energy to better things than lazing on the couch, than non-stop reading, than excessive television viewing. I wanted to be strong in character *and* in body. To be powerful in mind *and* in body. To be efficient, capable....Well, I wanted to be an asset to my family and to others. To be a woman of worth and excellence, a woman who is priceless.

I've shared my heart's desires. Now...how about yours?

A Godly Woman Is...Faithful

Proverbs 31:11

ecently I heard about a couple who exchanged their wedding vows on top of the Rock of Gibraltar, the famed rock island at the western entrance to the Mediterranean Sea. The groom explained that they wanted to found their marriage on a rock.

Well, far better for a husband than saying one's vows on the Rock of Gibraltar is establishing a marriage on the rock of Jesus Christ and the bedrock faithfulness of his wife! When a man marries a woman who is mentally, emotionally, physically, and spiritually strong, he can confidently build his life, his work, and his home, trusting in her rock-solid character to be a cornerstone for his efforts.

Such a woman was the godly woman of Proverbs 31. Let's discover another of her treasures—her faithfulness.

Discovering the Treasure....

Begin by reading Proverbs 31:10-31 in your personal Bible. Check here when done _____. Then write out verse 11.

1. *The heart*—As we approach the value of this woman of excellence, it helps to know that this verse does not refer to this husband's *affection for his wife,* but to his *confidence in his wife*—a "full confidence."[5] What do these proverbs say about the damage done by a wife with a character flaw?

   —Proverbs 12:4

   —Proverbs 19:13

   —Proverbs 21:9,19

   —Proverbs 27:15

2. *The trust*—Throughout the book of Proverbs God advises against trusting in anyone or anything other than God. For instance, what do these Proverbs warn?

—Proverbs 3:5

—Proverbs 11:28

—Proverbs 28:26

Now, what do these Proverbs teach us to do instead?

—Proverbs 3:5

—Proverbs 16:20

—Proverbs 28:25

—Proverbs 29:25

As you can see, normally we are to trust in God and not man. However, in this rare exception (Proverbs 31:11), the husband can also trust in his wife's faithfulness. Or, put another way, "the husband's heart *does not fear* because he feels confidence in and trust toward his wife."[6]

3. *The wife*—Verse 10 hinted at the dazzling excellence of this wonderful wife. But in verse 11 God begins to shine His spotlight on her magnificence. We've already noted that the masculine word for "virtuous" is used in the Bible to describe warriors. But here in verse 11 the Hebrew language paints "a metaphoric picture of this woman as a mighty warrior who utilizes her abilities for the benefit of her husband's domain."[7] Her commitment of all her resources—both mental and physical—is to the well-being of her husband and to his reputation. How does she better his life as shown in Proverbs 31:11?

And in verse 12?

And what is his reputation according to verse 23?

4. *Her contribution*—So far we've learned that the heart of this godly woman's husband trusts in her faithfulness. What additional blessing is described in verse 11?

"Spoil" or "gain" refers many times in the Bible to the booty or spoils or plunder taken in war by a conquering army. It was a risky way to attain income and wealth. What does the husband of the Proverbs 31 woman possess instead? And why will he not have to lie, cheat, and steal to increase his assets?

Developing Godly Excellence...

- *If you are married*—Can you point to any area of your life or any behavior that would cause your husband not to trust in you? Also note the changes you plan to make to be a more faithful wife.

  What have you learned a husband's greatest asset should be (verse 10)? Could the same be said of your contribution to your husband? Why or why not?

- *If you're not married*—Don't forget that the quality we're admiring in the Proverbs 31 woman is her faithfulness. How do you measure up on the faithfulness scale? Or put another way, how would those who know you best, who work with you, who live with you, rate you?

  Would you say that you are a valuable asset to those at home, at school, at work? That you are utterly dependable, trustworthy, and faithful? Why or why not?

A Heart in Pursuit of Excellence

As you can see, the Proverbs 31 woman is outstanding in that she was a faithful, loyal, and trustworthy woman of impeccable character and able management. As such, she was truly a woman of excellence and a blessing from God to those she served! Her devotion and godly conduct made this woman a stay and a source of confidence to others.

We cannot leave this shining treasure of faithfulness without a piercing, penetrating look in the mirror. We simply must examine our hearts as we pursue the excellence that is to mark us as God's women. Are you and I women of faithfulness? Can others—beginning with those at home—count on us? Can others trust us with information? With work? With responsibility? Can others place their confidence in us...no matter what? As yet another proverb so vividly says, "Confidence in an unfaithful man in time of trouble is like a bad tooth and a foot out of joint" (Proverbs 25:19).

Just like this faithful wife in Proverbs 31:11 who was the wealth and treasure of her husband, so you are to be to all who know you and to all whom you serve. Then dear one, the priceless gem of faithfulness will cause you to be truly worth *far more* than any treasure!

esson 5

A Godly Woman Is...Good

Proverbs 31:12

o you know what's at the heart of a godly woman, dear one? It's a heart of goodness that gives to others. Therefore...

> ...give because it is your role. Because of who
> God is, a woman after His heart is a woman who
> gives. As Christians we are to give, as wives we
> are to give, as mothers we are to give, as singles
> we are to give. That's our role, our assignment
> from God, as His children.[8]

The giver, dear one, is *you*. As one of God's treasured women you are meant to give and to do good, to deal out good, to operate out of a good heart, to be at work dispensing goodness, to routinely benefit others by your goodness.

Discovering the Treasure...

Begin by reading Proverbs 31:10-31 in your personal Bible. Check here when done _____. Then write out verse 12.

We already know that the heart of the Proverbs 31 woman's husband trusts in her (verse 11). But now God unveils the reason—"She does him good and not evil all the days of her life." This is quite a statement! (And wouldn't it be lovely to have this statement on *your* tombstone!)

1. *The gift*—God's most excellent wife clearly gives her husband the gift of goodness. Now, quickly, how do you witness the following wives doing evil to their husbands?

   —Eve (Genesis 2:18; 3:6)

   —David's wife Michal (2 Samuel 6:16)

   —Solomon's wives (1 Kings 11:4)

   —Jezebel (1 Kings 21:25)

2. *The giver*—Who is the giver of good deeds and acts of kindness in Proverbs 31:12?

Now meet a godly woman and wife who, despite her awful husband and difficult marriage, did her husband good. Her name was Abigail, and she's been referred to as "the good angel of Nabal's household."[9] You'll find her story in 1 Samuel 25.

Describe the man Nabal (verses 2-3,17,25,36).

Then describe his wife, Abigail (verse 3).

Briefly, what foolish decision did Nabal make (verses 4-12)?

And how did David respond (verses 13,21-22)?

Again, briefly, how did Abigail save the day, save her husband's life, and save his servants' lives, thus working good on behalf of Nabal's household (verses 18-19,23-27)?

What was the outcome of Abigail's wise thinking and quick actions (verses 32-33)?

3. *The extent*—How long did the noble woman and wife of Proverbs 31:12 dispense goodness?

What do you think this indicates about her heart and her character?

Developing Godly Excellence...

- *The Ultimate Giver*—What was a mark of Jesus' life and lifestyle according to Acts 10:38?

- *Your sphere*—Name those who populate the sphere of your everyday life (husband, children, parents, fellow workers, friends, neighbors, roommates). Then list several specific acts of kindness you can graciously bestow upon them with the Lord's help. (Caution: Remember that what you are at home is what you are! Practice goodness under your own roof first. Be sure your loved ones receive the first fruits of your goodness...all day long...every day...all the days of your life!)

- *Your goodness*—What changes of heart and mind will it require of you to make goodness your lifestyle? Answer below and then enjoy one of John Wesley's codes for his daily conduct.

*D*o all the good you can, by all the means you can,
in all the ways you can, in all the places you can,
at all the times you can, to all the people you can,
as long as ever you can.[10]

A Heart in Pursuit of Excellence

Beloved, goodness is a treasure you share with others, and, practically speaking, all we have is today. Therefore this is the day that counts for pursuing goodness and for dispensing it to others. Hear the heart of another regarding pursuing this most excellent trait of goodness:

*M*y life shall touch a dozen lives
     before this day is done,
Leave countless marks for good or ill
     ere sets the evening sun,
This is the wish I always wish,
     the prayer I always pray;
Lord, may my life help other lives
     it touches by the way.[11]

What is the prayer of your heart as you marvel over the treasure of the Proverbs 31 woman's goodness? Why not write it out and pray it now?

Lesson 6

A Godly Woman Is...Diligent

Proverbs 31:13

While researching the treasures of the godly Proverbs 31 woman, I discovered this glowing testimony by one Bible commentator about his own mother.

> My mother...span with both hands every afternoon; and as her eyes were not fully occupied with the work, she kept a Bible lying open on the "stock" of the wheel, that by a glance now and then she might feed her soul while she was employed in clothing her household.[12]

Wouldn't you like to have known this dear, sweet godly woman who sat, spun, and sought spiritual enlightenment all at the same time? She sounds like the woman of Proverbs 31 to me! Read on...!

Discovering the Treasure...

Begin by reading Proverbs 31:10-31 in your personal Bible. Check here when done _____. Then write out verse 13.

1. *The supplies*—Name the two materials the woman in Proverbs 31:13 diligently sought out and searched for.

   Once the raw materials were found, what steps (verse 19) still remained to prepare them for usefulness?

2. *The work*—A variety of translations of verse 13 reveal the flavor of both the Proverbs 31 woman's heart *and* her hands—she worked delightfully, with willing hands, working busily, and delighting to work. My particular favorite is "She puts her hands joyfully to the work."[13] What does your Bible say in verse 13?

   Other women in the Bible plied their hearts and their hands as they worked with wool and flax to benefit others. In each case, briefly note the particulars and the people who benefitted from the work of these godly women.

   —Exodus 35:25-26

   —1 Samuel 2:18-19

—Acts 9:39

3. *The weaving*—The result of the Proverbs 31 woman's diligence in searching for and working with wool and flax was a blessing to her family and to the community. How were her woven works put to use?

—verse 21

—verse 22

—verse 24

—and possibly in verse 20

Developing Godly Excellence...

- *Your heart*—The godly woman in Proverbs 31 actively and heartily sought and searched for wool and flax, the supplies she found and worked and used to bless her family and others. Her diligent efforts required energy, initiative, and the motivation of love. Take a minute to describe your heart and your energy, initiative, and motivational levels in the area of taking care of your family and doing the work of love. Are they nonexistent, low, so-so, sporadic, getting up there, or high? Pick one and then explain what caused you to evaluate your heart and hands in this way.

Now, what can you do, in the words of the popular TV chef Emeril, to "kick it up a notch"?

- *Your work*—Once her materials were acquired, God's woman of excellence went to work. Again, according to verse 13, how did she work, and what was the attitude of her heart?

As you consider these scriptures, state in a few words what principles are taught regarding work.

—Proverbs 10:4

—Proverbs 14:23

—Proverbs 28:19

List at least three ways you can become a better worker. When I first went through this exercise (about 25 years ago!) I came up with these three answers:

1) Study time management books.

2) Force myself to get up from my couch.

3) Make a daily schedule.

Now, my friend, what will your answers be?

1)

2)

3)

A Heart in Pursuit of Excellence

Dear one, it's a joy to discover how this godly woman's excellent work of weaving blessed and benefitted others. Truly, her diligence resulted in both literal weavings and the masterful weaving called *home*. And we can only imagine the pleasure she derived personally as she worked diligently with her hands and joyfully in her heart. As the age-old maxim teaches us,

~ A willing heart lightens work. ~

We've beheld the workmanship of the Proverbs 31 woman. Now...how about you? What is your "weaving" producing? Is it worthy to hang in the halls of heaven?

Lesson 7

A Godly Woman Is…Enterprising

s we step into this next quality at the heart of God's woman of excellence, all I can say is…watch out! The godly woman of Proverbs 31 is in motion! Her wheels are turning! Stay out of her way and give her a wide berth! Why? Because, as one scholar has noted, "an established factor within the woman's character results in a continuing activity."[14]

Let's look at her *and* at her enterprising activities!

Discovering the Treasure…

Begin by reading Proverbs 31:10-31 in your personal Bible. Check here when done _____. Then write out verse 14.

1. *The picture*—What is God's priceless woman likened to in Proverbs 31, verse 14?

   What items might she have been procuring on her shopping outings according to...

   ...verse 13?

   ...verse 16?

   ...verse 18?

   In the book of Proverbs, wisdom is personified as an enterprising woman. What efforts do these verses picture?

   —Proverbs 9:1-2

   —Proverbs 14:1

   —Proverbs 24:3-4

   —Proverbs 31:27

2. *Her provision*—Both the merchant ships *and* this enterprising woman transported items "from afar." However, whereas a ship brings its cargo toward *a port,* God's enterprising woman brings hers toward *home.* What kinds of cargo?

In verse 13, this lady actively sought _____.

Now in verse 14, she seeks _____.

Using your dictionary, jot down a working definition of the word *enterprising.*

3. *Her enterprising spirit*—Other women in the Bible show us the treasure of an enterprising spirit. What energetic and enterprising qualities do you witness in...

...Rebekah in Genesis 24:15-20?

...Rachel in Genesis 29:9?

...Ruth (Ruth 2:2-3 and 17-18)?

Developing Godly Excellence...

• *The picture*—Think about the image of a sailing ship and of a "sailing" woman as she runs her daily errands. What do you think "puts the wind in her sails" as she runs to and fro to gather up goods?

Are there any course adjustments you need to make in the set of your "sails" that would help you to better follow in the wake of this godly woman in the areas of energy, eagerness, and enterprise? Please explain your answer.

- *Your provision*—God's Proverbs 31 homemaker brought "food" from afar for her family and "household" (verse 15). In her mind and heart the effort was obviously worth it...and it should be for us too! I remember reading a book that recommended that you and I prepare as much of the evening meal as possible first thing in the morning. The wise author suggested that women make this #1 way of serving their family #1 on the daily to-do list. How do you think such a practice would help you to better provide food for your family? And how do you think it might better the quality of the food and dinners you serve?

- *Your enterprising spirit*—In your opinion and from your own experience as a homemaker, what might some of the character qualities be that produce the enterprising efforts like those revealed in the Proverbs 31 woman?

Married or single, make a list of your daily duties and responsibilities. What is your current attitude toward those duties and responsibilities? Please be honest.

Now, how can you take a page out of God's enterprising woman's book and improve your attitude? Also list any favorite scriptures that can assist you.

A Heart in Pursuit of Excellence

No heart will pursue excellence without first of all that heart being a heart of love. As the Bible teaches us, without love we are "nothing" (1 Corinthians 13:2). And, dear one, without love we will *want* to do nothing!

We've only just begun discovering the variety of projects the Proverbs 31 woman of excellence pursued. And what do you think created, drove, and guided her enterprising spirit? In a word, it was *love!* Love for others and love for home.

Now, how's your heart of love?

Lesson 8

A Godly Woman Is...Disciplined

Proverbs 31:15

One of my favorite childhood memories is the time spent each summer on my uncle's ranch in West Texas. Being a city girl, I was thrilled to ride the range on horseback. But my time on the ranch was also marked by being exposed to the incredible daily discipline and work ethic of my uncle, aunt, and cousins. To begin the list of disciplines, they got up early! *Very* early! I mean in-the-dark early! And so I did too, accompanying and assisting them as they fed chickens, gathered eggs, milked and fed the cows, and cleaned their stalls.

Whenever I read Proverbs 31:15, I can relate to the disciplines highlighted in it because of my firsthand exposure to such a lifestyle.

Discovering the Treasure...

Begin by reading Proverbs 31:10-31 in your personal Bible. Check here when done _____. Then write out verse 15.

1. *Her schedule*—What is the first thing we learn about the schedule of God's Proverbs 31 woman?

As you consider the remainder of verse 15, what can you surmise were some of her reasons for early rising?

Name some others in the Bible who are noted for early rising. Note their reasons for this discipline.

—Genesis 19:27

—Psalm 5:3

—Mark 1:35

—Luke 24:1

2. *Her family*—How did the godly woman, wife, and mother of Proverbs 31 serve her family at this early hour?

Who else did she take care of (verse 15)?

Just a note—The Hebrew word used here for "food" actually means *prey* and refers to the prey of a lion. Not only is this godly woman like a warrior (verse 10), a worker (verse 13), and a fleet of merchant ships (verse 14), but she's also a lioness who feeds her own.[15]

3. *Her plan*—Verse 15 is the only verse in this passage from Proverbs 31 that contains three lines. Technically, it's called a *triplet*. How does the third line in your Bible read?

The Proverbs 31 woman rose early not only to feed her family and her maidens, but to assign them their duties for the day. She gave her maidens their "portion" or "task," meaning whatever is appointed.[16] In other words, they received their instructions and work chores for the day. Clearly this wise and disciplined woman got up early, made a plan, and then delegated the day's work to her helpers and to herself. What do these scriptures teach us about the wisdom of planning and organizing?

—Proverbs 16:3

—Proverbs 21:5

What caution should we take as we approach our grand plans according to James 4:13-15?

Developing Godly Excellence...

- *Your schedule*—Just as ships "rise" on the sea (Proverbs 31:14), God's faithful woman also "rises" early.[17] Take a minute now to remember and describe a morning that started up before you did! Then describe one when you were the first one up. What were some of the differences?

- *Your early rising*—Of course there are exceptions and reasons why we sometimes don't get up early, but what is it that usually keeps you from being an early riser?

- *Your plan*—What steps can you take to make headway on establishing the pattern of getting up a little earlier? List at least three.

Step 1—

Step 2—

Step 3—

A Heart in Pursuit of Excellence

The Proverbs 31 woman put the needs of the day and of others above herself and her personal comfort. Faithful to others and to her responsibilities, she rose early to get the jump on the day. Truly she knew well that nothing of importance is ever done without a plan. Grand things don't just *happen!*

Dear sister, do you know how to have a successful and productive day? Just pursue the excellent pattern of the godly woman of Proverbs 31. She heartily sought and developed the disciplines in the...

> practice of early rising,
>
> provision of daily food, and
>
> planning of the day's work

Who knows what we could accomplish for God, give to others, and realize for ourselves if only we would follow in this godly woman's disciplined footsteps!

*L*esson 9

A Godly Woman Is...Thrifty
Proverbs 31:16

*N*ow that Jim and I live in the country, one major high-light of every month is when I finally get to visit my local dis-count store (you know the scene—the kind of discount store that is basically a sprawling warehouse!). I wait all month long...and then, at last, the day arrives when I take my long list and make the one-hour trek to the nearest warehouse. Oh how I love walking up and down each and every aisle looking for what I need according to my shopping list. But I also keep a keen eye out for what might be a bargain. I mean, I even go down the pet aisle...and I don't even have a pet! But there just might be some other bargain item at the end of the shelves.

However, my idea of thrift pales in comparison to our wise and thrifty Proverbs 31 lady. Let's see what she's up to in this lesson as we discover yet another of the many treasures of her godly character.

Discovering the Treasure...

Begin by reading Proverbs 31:10-31 in your personal Bible. Check here when done _____. Then write out verse 16.

1. *Her mental pattern*—At the base of this woman's thrift is a mental habit. What did she do first when she perhaps heard that a local field had come up for sale, and what does this indicate about her thrift and mental pattern?

2. *Her financial preparations*—What was her next action, and what does this indicate about her thrift and financial preparations?

3. *Her physical abilities*—What other action do we discover in this godly woman, and what does it indicate about her thrift and physical abilities?

Just a note for better understanding—"field" and "vineyard" are different words for distinctly different kinds of property. This woman did not purchase a field and then plant a vineyard there, but rather she purchases both a field and a vineyard.[18] This, in essence, doubles the efforts and actions we witness here.

Developing Godly Excellence...

- *Your mental considerations*—When it comes to shopping and spending money, are you prone to making rash decisions and impulsive purchases, or are you one who waits and carefully "considers" your purchases? Please describe your habits.

    What do you think is involved in "considering" a purchase before you buy? And how do you think this one mental practice would aid you in the Thrift Department?

- *Your financial preparations*—This woman bought a field. As one Bible scholar comments on this statement, "There is no way we can interpret this to say less than what is obvious. This woman apparently does buy and sell land...."[19] What does this reveal about her financial thrift and preparations? And how do you think her example would aid you in the Savings Department?

- *Your physical abilities*—Next our lady personally and physically—with her own hands—planted a vineyard. Look again at verse 13 of Proverbs 31. Once again, *how* did this woman work? What do you think this indicates about her attitude toward her work, even physical work? Also what do you think contributes to such an attitude, and do you think your attitude measures up? How do you think her example—and a few changes—would help you in the Work Department?

A Heart in Pursuit of Excellence

How do dreams become reality? The progression for the godly woman of Proverbs 31 went like this:

Her virtue (verse 10) led to
  her willing heart (verse 13) which led to
    her industry (verse 13) which led to
      her savings (verse 11) which led to
        her investments (verse 16) which led to
          her prosperity (verse 25).[20]

Behind every success story is plain ol' hard work—powered by love for others, a vision of their well-being, a dream about how to make that happen, a heart in pursuit of excellence, and God's gracious blessing!

Lesson 10

A Godly Woman Is...Energetic

Proverbs 31:17

oday's lesson reminds me of two contrasting pictures of feminine strength and physical fitness. My first picture comes from getting off an elevator on the wrong floor of a hotel and observing a health and beauty spa in full action. The women on that floor were "wòrking out" by having their bodies pampered with muds, wraps, oils, and every kind of beauty treatment imaginable!

My other picture of women at work comes from the land of Israel. There I saw women truly working, for they were harvesting wheat in hot, golden fields of ripe grain. With their flowing robes tucked tight through their legs and cinched into a belt or sash, they were hard at work cutting, bundling, and carrying wheat uphill to a threshing area where they proceeded to beat out their grain and then toss it into the air with pitchforks. It was quite a sight!

As we begin this lesson on both physical and mental strength, let's make sure we keep the *second* picture—the women in Israel—in mind, for that image, dear one, is more like how the godly woman of Proverbs developed her strength.

Discovering the Treasure...

Begin by reading Proverbs 31:10-31 in your personal Bible. Check here when done _____. Then write out verse 17.

1. *Remembering*—Think back to what we discovered in Lesson 3 about the meaning of "virtuous" or "excellent." This word described and pictured the excellent woman of Proverbs 31 as a female "warrior" who was strong in body and in spirit. How do you see this description lived out in Proverbs 31:17?

2. *Her mental energy*—The words in verse 17, oh so carefully chosen by the teacher of Proverbs 31, suggest *the attitude toward work*. Looking again at verse 13, what was her attitude toward work?

What additional boosts in attitude can a woman tap into according to these verses?

—Nehemiah 8:10

—Ecclesiastes 9:10

—Psalm 118:24

—Proverbs 14:23

—Galatians 5:22

—Philippians 4:13

3. *Her physical energy*—Next the teacher of this alphabetical acrostic points in verse 17 to *the ability to work*. God's Proverbs 31 woman is strong. Why?

Developing Godly Excellence...

• *Your mental energy*—List a handful of practices that are proven to increase a person's mental energy. Are you failing in any one of them? If so, what can—or must!— you do to "gird" yourself with greater mental strength and energy?

- *Your physical energy*—List a handful of practices that are proven to increase a person's physical energy. Are you failing in any one of them? If so, what can—or must!—you do to "gird" yourself with greater physical strength and energy?

A Heart in Pursuit of Excellence

As I write about this gleaming treasure of energy discovered in this godly woman after God's own heart—both her mental and physical energy—I'm having three thoughts.

First of all, *I* want more energy! Life is wondrously full and so precious as it arrives each new day brimming over with fresh opportunities to grow and to be used by God to serve others. If only I had more energy!

Next, I'm also thinking of my cherished daughter Katherine, who is down for a month after back surgery. Yet, while lacking physical energy, Katherine is masterfully managing her household that's complete with a husband and two preschoolers. I know there are times and circumstances that prevent our having the physical prowess we long for. But we can still put our mental energy to use!

Finally, I'm realizing that I need to continue (and in some cases, reinstate!) the daily disciplines that enhance both my mental and physical energy.

What thoughts are you having, dear reading sister? How would more energy affect your daily life? How would it affect the daily lives of those around you? And what will you do today to pursue a heart—and body and mind—of excellence?

esson 11

A Godly Woman Is...Industrious

little night work." That's what I call the activity high-lighted in this verse.[21] This is the type of work a woman does in the evening when she's tired and wants to go to bed but still has things that must get done. God's Proverbs 31 woman helps us discover yet another godly virtue as we learn that, seldom idle, her industry continues on into the night.

Let's peek into her lamp-lit window and witness firsthand what she does after dark.

Discovering the Treasure...

Begin by reading Proverbs 31:10-31 in your personal Bible. Check here when done _____. Then write out verse 18.

1. *Her evaluation*—We can almost sense the surprise or classic spark of an idea as "the light goes on" for this woman as she "perceives" that her merchandise or gain is "good." The word "perceive" is the same Hebrew word that is translated "taste" in Psalm 34:8. What did the psalmist "taste" and "perceive" in Psalm 34:8?

   And what did this most excellent woman taste and perceive in Proverbs 31:18?

2. *Her merchandise*—As you scan through Proverbs 31:10-31 again, how many sources or kinds of merchandise do you find in the items she bought, secured, labored over, traded, and turned into savings, income, or gain for her household?

3. *Her efforts*—As a result of recognizing that her efforts were good and excellent and fruitful, what did the woman of Proverbs 31 do next?

To review her efforts, what does this woman's morning, daytime, and evening work schedule look like according to…

…verse 15?

…verse 16?

…verse 18?

Are you squirming? Well, take heart! The culture and the climate of this lady's homeland of Palestine called for a downtime or nap time during the heat of the day. Nevertheless, what picture is emerging of this woman's industry and work ethic, and why (verse 18)?

Developing Godly Excellence…

- *Your evaluation*—What is it that you love to do and excel at? Or put another way, are you receiving compliments for something you do? What is it?

- *Your merchandise*—We considered some of the ways the godly woman of Proverbs 31 contributed to the well-being of others. How about you? How are you blessing and benefitting others by your wise management and willing work?

- *Your efforts*—We've already referred to food guru Emeril and his advice to constantly be "kicking it up a notch." Once again, what did the Proverbs 31 woman do to "kick up" her efforts a notch or two?

Now, how can you do the same in terms of…

…time?

…effort?

…commitment?

A Heart in Pursuit of Excellence

Caring, creative, and confident. These are three words that most definitely describe the treasured woman of Proverbs 31! She possessed a heart that cared deeply for the things of the Lord and for people. As she worked industriously, her creative abilities blossomed and her skills grew until the end product of her efforts was excellent. Finally, her skills and confidence bloomed, so much so that she gladly turned up the heat of her efforts to do what brought joy to her heart and blessing to her loved ones and others. As you and I put our confidence in the Lord, labor out of a full and joyful heart, work hard (and late!), and grow in the areas of our gifts, abilities, and skills, we, too, will discover the treasure of doing things well, of benefitting others, and of spending our precious time and energy in delightful, rewarding ways. What joy!

Lesson 12

A Godly Woman Is...Persistent

Emilie Barnes has long been a source of encouragement for me and millions of other struggling Proverbs-31-wannabes who pore over her many timesaving books for busy, disorganized women. In fact, her ministry is called More Hours in My Day. If anyone could get more hours out of her day, Emilie is at the top of the list!

In this lesson we meet the highly persistent woman who is the ultimate originator of the "More Hours in My Day Club." She is, once again, the godly woman of Proverbs 31. Do you want to have more hours in your day? Do you want to be as persistent and productive as the Proverbs 31 woman (and as an Emilie Barnes)? Then peer once again into the window of God's feminine dynamo and see what she's up to. This next verse gives us a hint about what it will mean to follow the model of persistence witnessed in the woman of

Proverbs 31 and to follow the recommendation of one time management expert who advises,

~ Make your evenings and weekends count.[22] ~

Discovering the Treasure...

Begin by reading Proverbs 31:10-31 in your personal Bible. Check here when done _____. Then write out verse 19.

1. *Her evenings*—Look again at Proverbs 31:18. How did God's treasured woman of Proverbs 31 spend some of her time in the evenings?

2. *Her activities*—According to verse 19, what could several of her night activities have been?

_____

_____

3. *Her persistence*—The two ancient objects—the distaff and the spindle—are rarely mentioned in the Old Testament. We know that they were used for spinning wool (verse

13) and were the tools of the cloth-making trade for the Proverbs 31 woman. What were some of the outcomes of her skills and persistence at the spinning wheel as seen in...

...verse 17?

...verse 21?

...verse 22?

...verse 24?

Developing Godly Excellence...

- *Your evenings*—I know that before I discovered this excellent woman and her example of persistence (even in the evening!), I generally spent my evenings plopped on the couch in front of the television with a bowl of Cheetos and a Coke. And then I found Proverbs 31 and the godly woman pictured there...which led to some serious adjustments! How do you normally spend your evenings? Describe the scene here...hour by hour.

Are there any changes you must make to follow in the footsteps of God's woman of persistence and productivity? List at least three improvements you will make.

_____

_____

_____

* *Your activities*—Begin praying about the people in your life—family, friends, workmates, those at church, the needy (verse 20). What activities could you pursue in the evenings that would better and bless their lives?

A Heart in Pursuit of Excellence

Truly, learning to use your evenings is like discovering hidden treasure! And it's a treasure you can share with others!

Our family was blessed by one of God's women who bettered our lives by using the treasure of her evenings to do "a little night work." Her name was Dorothy Johnson, and Jim was her Sunday school pastor. Dorothy was a senior citizen who lived alone and chose, rather than withdrawing and pining away in her sunset years, to crochet beautiful items for those she loved and for those in need. I wish you could see all the handmade, created-with-love works she showered upon us (a needy seminary family in very lean years)! We have booties, bed socks, lap shawls, afghans, and blanket throws that grace our home and warm our bodies.

And, beloved, we were not the only ones Dorothy ministered to with her efforts. She regularly mailed off boxes to missionaries around the world. And those in our church who were homebound, in nursing homes, or ill at home regularly received her handmade goods.

Do you know where Dorothy Johnson was when she went to heaven to meet her Lord face to face? She was in her favorite chair, with her table lamp lit...crocheting during yet another evening alone. She was thinking of others, doing for others, and, knowing Dorothy, probably praying for others as she worked with her hands.

Don't you agree that Dorothy provides you and me with a perfect—and poignant—picture of Proverbs 31, verses 18 and 19? Dorothy was a true woman after God's own heart who used her hours (even the hours of her night!) persisting and plying her skills to better the lives of others. Discovering and using more hours in her day by utilizing the hours of her night served to benefit more people...including me. I am indeed most blessed to have known such a godly woman!

A Godly Woman Is...Kind

Proverbs 31:20

*P*ractically every female alive—young or old—has heard of the name Florence Nightingale. This woman almost single-handedly revolutionized nursing. Before Miss Nightingale's reforms, nurses were largely untrained personnel. However, through her efforts the stature of nursing was raised to a medical profession with high standards of education. Nursing is a noble profession today because this one woman stretched out her kind hands and heart to help the needy. Through the years following her efforts, Florence Nightingale has inspired countless others to follow in her merciful footsteps.

In this lesson we meet another woman who is known for her kindness. But before we do, enjoy these lines by American poet Henry Wadsworth Longfellow, which were inspired by the legend of Florence Nightingale as "The Lady of the Lamp."

A lady with a lamp shall stand
In the great history of the land,
A noble type of good,
Heroic womanhood.

Discovering the Treasure...

Begin by reading Proverbs 31:10-31 in your personal Bible.
Check here when done _____. Then write out verse 20.

1. *Her hand*—Once again, what did the godly woman do
   with her "hand" (singular)?

   This lovely image of the single extended hand reveals this
   woman's kind and generous nature. For instance, if money
   is what some poor person needs, she reaches into her
   purse and shares her wealth. If bread is needed, she
   reaches into her pantry and passes on a golden loaf. If
   warm clothes are missing, she provides one of her own
   handmade woolen coats (verse 21).

2. *Her hands*—What did the godly woman do with her
   "hands" (plural)?

Here the image expands to include both hands. Nursing the sick, for instance, requires two hands. So does caring for babies, young children, and the elderly.

3. *Her heart*—This woman's heart is involved too. The verbs "extends" and "reaches out" suggest that her giving stretches as far as her means will allow.[23] What do these scriptures tell us that God desires to be at the core of our hearts?

—Deuteronomy 15:7-8

—Proverbs 11:25

—Proverbs 19:17

—Proverbs 22:9

—Micah 6:8

Developing Godly Excellence...

- *Your hands*—Not only have you heard of Florence Nightingale, but you've probably also heard this saying— "Idle hands are the devil's workshop." As we're learning from our study of Proverbs 31 and the godly woman portrayed there, it's good to stay busy. So pray and ask God what you can do to roll up your sleeves and extend your hands and your kindness in these areas:

  The giving of money—

  The giving of food—

  The giving of assistance—

  The giving of help to the elderly or the ill—

- *Your heart*—How do these "Sisters in Mercy" encourage you to a greater heart of kindness and compassion?

  —The widow of Zarephath (1 Kings 17:8-16)

  —The Shunammite woman (2 Kings 4:8-11)

—Dorcas (Acts 9:36-39)

—The Proverbs 31 woman (verse 20)

A Heart in Pursuit of Excellence

There's no doubt about it—the Proverbs 31 woman used her hands for ministry. She wasn't afraid to roll up her sleeves and touch those who were suffering. In fact, her great heart of love compelled her kindness. Whatever the need, she held out her hands—her literal, open, upturned palms—to offer any helpful items or helpful services.

So how can you and I begin to pursue a heart of kindness? Here's a short to-do list for both of us—

Begin at home.

Keep your eyes and ears open (Proverbs 20:12).

Pray for a heart of love.

Err on the side of generosity.

These few practices, dear sister in mercy, will propel us down the path of developing a heart that is kind.

Lesson 14

A Godly Woman Is...Farsighted

Proverbs 31:21

*L*iving in mild, sunny Southern California for 30 years sure lulled me into complacency with respect to the possibility of disaster. So when "The Big One" hit on January 17, 1994, with its 6.8 epicenter three miles from our house, my family and I were definitely not prepared! Water, gas, electric, and phone were knocked out in a split second...and we didn't even have a flashlight! Thanks to organizations like the Red Cross, we finally obtained drinking water. Yes, we were unprepared for the next few weeks of no utilities, no services, and no open stores for purchasing food and water.

That earthquake served as a serious wake-up call on being better prepared for possible future emergencies. On the other hand, if the Proverbs 31 lady had been in my slippers (oops—I had no slippers nearby that early morning!) on that fateful day at 4 A.M.ish, she would have been prepared. She might have said, "Bring it on! I'm ready!" What would make her able to say such a thing? Let's find out now.

Discovering the Treasure...

Begin by reading Proverbs 31:10-31 in your personal Bible. Check here when done _____. Then write out verse 21.

1. *Her attitude*—What threatening weather condition was a possibility for this woman and her loved ones?

And what was her attitude toward such a possibility?

Why?

2. *Her preparations*—There are other evidences of this wise woman's farsighted preparations here in Proverbs 31. What are they as seen in...

...verse 15?

...verse 27?

What do the following scriptures teach us about the wisdom of preparation?

—Proverbs 6:6-8

—Proverbs 10:5

—Proverbs 27:23-27

3. *Her provision*—Look again at this woman's activities. Where do you think her family's clothing came from according to these scriptures...and who do you think made their garments?

—Proverbs 31:13

—Proverbs 31:19

—Proverbs 31:22

—Proverbs 31:24

For our information, "scarlet" or "red" indicates warmth, quality, and cost. Such a vivid color gave a stately appearance, was double-dipped into the crimson dye, and was possibly even double-thick. What do you think this suggests about this amazing woman's care for her loved ones?

4. *Another example*—Look again at Dorcas in Acts 9:36-39. What did this godly and farsighted (and kind and generous!) woman do, and for whom?

Developing Godly Excellence...

- *Your preparations*—List now some of the future preparations you can or must make for your household. As you look at the calendar for the upcoming year, what needs do you anticipate?

Are you prepared for bad weather and/or emergencies? What might such threats be, and how have or can you better prepare?

- A quick glance at this verse might give the impression that it's not very "meaty." Yet how many character qualities can you list that go into the preparations and provision made by this treasure of a woman...

    ...mentally?

    ...physically?

    ...creatively?

- *Your attitude*—What does Psalm 46:1-2 say is a godly woman's first and final source of help in time of need?

A Heart in Pursuit of Excellence

An entire lesson on bad weather, clothing, and preparations? This may not seem terribly important, but, dear one, it's about yet another fine virtue of this woman who is our model for life.

As we pursue a heart of excellence, realize that the work of preparation is important to God and that He will guide your planning. After all, He provides for us. His very name is *Jehovah-jireh,* "God will provide"! You and I have the opportunity to mirror this aspect of God's character when we plan and prepare in order to provide for our loved ones. Blessed by your farsighted preparations and by God's promised care, your loved ones are indeed doubly blessed!

Lesson 15

A Godly Woman Is...Elegant

Proverbs 31:22

My brother Richard lives and works in the hub of America's capital, Washington, D.C. Once when we visited him, Richard treated Jim and me to a tour of the Smithsonian. This famous museum is a vast structure with acres of exhibits. But the one that stole my heart that day was the display of the inaugural ball gowns of our presidential wives. I strolled slowly, stared intently, and took part in an hour-long audio tour. The dresses were most definitely fitting for the stature and position of our country's First Ladies.

Fitting. That's the word we want to key in on as we look now at the First Lady of the Bible, the Proverbs 31 woman. Let's take note of her home and of her wardrobe.

Discovering the Treasure...

Begin by reading Proverbs 31:10-31 in your personal Bible. Check here when done _____. Then write out verse 22.

1. *Her home*—In Proverbs 31:21 this farsighted woman carefully prepared and lovingly made woolen garments for her family. Now what do we find her making?

2. *Her industry*—The first half of this verse does not refer to clothing. Rather it is commenting on this exalted woman's home furnishings. In fact, the "coverings of tapestry" have been translated as carpets, woven coverlets, upholstery, and even quilts.[24] What do you think her activity in this verse portrays about this woman's...

   ...skills?

   ...abilities?

   ...use of time?

   ...home?

   ...heart?

3. *Her appearance*—Finally! At last we catch our first—and only!—glimpse of this godly woman. What do we learn about her?

Just a note regarding "silk"—Although a few English translations of Proverbs report that her clothing is made of silk, it is probably linen imported from Egypt, and "purple" describes the dyed fabric from Phoenicia.[25]

What kind of picture and impression do you imagine she created as our admirable lady of Proverbs 31 walked the streets of her sun-drenched city? (Be generous with your adjectives!)

Developing Godly Excellence...

- *Your home*—God allows us to see firsthand in Proverbs 31:22 the decor of our splendid woman's home and the items she lovingly made and furnished it with. Now, my friend, what would others see as they enter your home? Is it one that sends a message that someone cares...or is it the opposite? Please describe the first impressions your physical place may be sending out.

- *Your industry*—The emphasis in Proverbs 31 is not about wealth and luxury. It's about care and beauty and the time spent creating that beauty. Take a walk through your dwelling place, whether that place is half a dorm room, one bedroom in a shared apartment, a flat, or a house. What can you do to *deck* (the literal meaning of the word "makes"[26]) out your home? Try writing down one improvement you can make in each room. (And, I repeat, this exercise is not about spending money! It's about spending time, effort, and care.)

- *Your clothing*—There's another side to our clothing that's even more important and valuable than our appearance. What do the following passages reveal about God's standards for beauty and for your clothing and appearance?

—Proverbs 31:30

—2 Corinthians 4:16

—1 Timothy 2:9-10

—1 Peter 3:3-4

Are there any changes you need to make to better walk in the pattern God sets for His women? Be specific.

A Heart in Pursuit of Excellence

What a joy—and a privilege—you and I have as God presents us with daily opportunities to express ourselves creatively in the beauty of our home and our clothing! Wherever home is, we can "weave" a tapestry of beauty there. Why, we can even transform a camper into a warm and welcoming home.

And then there is our appearance. I like the thought of this hardworking woman strolling elegantly through the streets of her town in her fine attire. Certainly she was neither overdressed nor extravagant, but, given her character, she wore what was appropriate and fitting of a godly, queenly woman who reveled in the fact that she was the daughter of the King of the universe.

Surely you and I can take a page out of this woman's book! Surely we can pursue her excellence by paying attention to the visual beauty of our homes and our appearance!

esson 16

A Godly Woman Is...Helpful

*H*ave you ever thought much about your influence on others? The helpful support you give to others many times makes it possible for them to be successful in their ventures.

In this lesson we observe a man of influence. He's the fortunate husband of the Proverbs 31 woman. And by all accounts, he's successful. Indeed, he is a wise counselor and a man of influence in his community. (And why wouldn't he be with the treasure of a Proverbs 31 wife to help him?!)

Do you want others to succeed, especially those closest to you—whether your family and husband or those at church or work? Then your contribution to their success can be as simple as the help you give out of the treasure of a selfless heart.

Discovering the Treasure...

Begin by reading Proverbs 31:10-31 in your personal Bible. Check here when done _____. Then write out verse 23.

1. *The husband*—So far, what have we learned about the husband of the Proverbs 31 woman...

   ...in verse 11?

   ...in verse 12?

   Now what do we learn in verse 23 about his status and service in his community?

2. *The gates*—In the days of the Proverbs 31 woman, cities were walled around for protection. Gated entrances containing large rooms were built into the city wall. What are some of the activities that went on in "the gates" according to these verses?

   —Ruth 4:1-5

   —2 Samuel 15:1-2

—Esther 2:21-23

3. *The elders*—Who were the companions and colleagues of the Proverbs 31 husband?

Just a note—The "elders" were the members of the judicial body that ruled the land. This prestigious group met daily in the town gate to transact any public business or decide cases that were brought before them.[27]

Developing Godly Excellence...

- *A man's influence*—Think of some helpful ways a wife can contribute to her husband's usefulness or to others on the job and in the community. List several here.

- *A man's mate*—Can you think of any wives in the Bible who hindered their husband's reputation and ability to serve others well? Name a few and write out a brief summary of their negative influence.

Hearts in Pursuit of Excellence

Dear one, the excellent wife of Proverbs 31 served as a bookend to her husband. As a matched set they worked together to serve God and others.

- He contributes to the community; she is his helpmeet (Genesis 2:18).

- He is successful in the realm of city management; she is successful in the realm of family and home management.

- He is happy at work; she is happy working at home.

- He is respected and held in high esteem; she preserves and advances his honor by her conduct and example.

- He is deferred to as a solid, influential citizen; she brings credit to him.

- He is a counselor, a man of common sense and not-so-common insight; she speaks with loving wisdom.

- He exerts his influence on the life of the community in the city gates; she influences the community from home.

- He is known for his solid character and important contributions; so is she.

- He has achieved some worldly wealth and social status; she improves his financial situation as well as his social standing by what she is to him and what she does for him as a wife.

- He has reached his professional aims; she has helped him do so by her diligence and frugality.

- He has earned prestige; she is respected for her creative handiwork.

- He is a virtuous man; she is a virtuous woman.

- He is crowned with honor; she is his crown (Proverbs 12:4).[28]

*esson 17

A Godly Woman Is...Creative

*I*n the beginning God created..." (Genesis 1:1). The very first words in the Bible describe our great and mighty God as One who created and thus was creative. But as an added bonus, my friend, you and I have been "created...in His own image" (Genesis 1:27). This means we possess some of God's attributes, and one of those attributes is creativity. Do you realize that each time you create something, you are saying to everyone, "I am creative because my God is creative, and I am made in His image"?

As we start a new lesson on the Proverbs 31 woman, we are again struck with her creative and industrious abilities. Let's look in on our imaginative teacher and discover yet another lesson in godliness.

Discovering the Treasure...

Begin by reading Proverbs 31:10-31 in your personal Bible. Check here when done _____. Then write out verse 24.

1. *Her industry*—Prior to this verse, we've witnessed God's Proverbs 31 woman in a variety of activities. Note these specific ones now.

   —Verse 13

   —Verse 19

   —Verse 21

   —Verse 22

   What do all of these activities seem to have in common?

   And now in verse 24 what three facts about her life do we learn?

   _____

   _____

   _____

2. *Her creativity*—What do the details in verse 24 reveal about this most excellent woman's creativity?

Just a note of information—This woman made her "linen" fabric first, *then* made garments out of it. And the "sashes" were like a belt or girdle, worn to gather the flowing garments of her day. Leather belts were common, but a linen sash or belt was more attractive and more costly, sometimes woven with gold and silver thread and studded with jewels and gold.

3. *Her "industry"*—This woman sold, bartered, and traded her fine linen and her exquisite sashes. In other words, she had a little industry going. What does this indicate about...

...the quality of her goods?

...the betterment of her family?

...an outlet for her creativity?

Developing Godly Excellence...

• *Your industry*—It's tempting to look at this godly woman and say, "But I don't have the free time she obviously had! How else could she accomplish all this?" But we know the truth, don't we? God's woman treasured her time...and she used it wisely and industriously. We've already addressed the hidden pockets of time that are available each day to women like you and me. What are two of those hidden pockets according to...

...verse 15?

...verse 18?

How are you doing when it comes to putting these two ends of the day to work for you and your loved ones? Please explain.

- *Your choices*—Beloved, we are most generally in charge of the choices we make. What are some of those choices illustrated in these proverbs, and what principle(s) does each teach us?

  —Proverbs 6:9-11

  —Proverbs 10:4

  —Proverbs 12:11

  —Proverbs 14:23

—Proverbs 18:9

—Proverbs 28:19

—Proverbs 31:27

• *Your creativity*—It makes sense that the more this dear woman wove clothing for her family and furnishings for her home, the better she got at it! And soon she excelled at her creative efforts. What do we learn about her and her goods in verse 18?

What is it that you do well...and love doing? I know I've asked this question before, but I want you to think, to pray, and to answer it again.

• *Your growth*—Are you faithful to improve your areas of giftedness and to increase your skills? What two things can you do to fuel your creative expertise?

_____

_____

A Heart in Pursuit of Excellence

I know we're busy women, but so was the godly woman in Proverbs 31. And here she shows us the way to manage our time and our lives so that we can pursue our passions without neglecting our work and those at home.

> She used her time
> (and somehow I think that's every *second* of it!),
> She planned and prepared for her activities,
> She followed a schedule, and
> She worked hard.

This, dear one, is a recipe we can both follow to the letter. So let's take some initiative. Let's get the creative juices flowing!

esson 18

A Godly Woman Is...Confident

Proverbs 31:25

y husband, Jim, has worn many hats and worked in many professions over the years. While wearing the hat of a Reserve Army Medical Corps officer, Jim spent time fulfilling his profession as a registered pharmacist while on active duty in a medical hospital in southern Germany during the Bosnian crisis in the late 1990s. While serving there in the picturesque rolling hills of Bavaria, Jim observed that the majority of the outpatient prescriptions dispensed were for anxiety, panic disorders, depression, and insomnia. These people certainly had little confidence in the future and required prescription drugs to face the future.

Now, dear one, contrast that grim scene with the Proverbs 31 woman who "smiles at the future." What is her secret?! Read on....

Discovering the Treasure...

Begin by reading Proverbs 31:10-31 in your personal Bible. Check here when done _____. Then write out verse 25.

1. *Her clothing of godly character*—What two prized ornaments of godliness clothe the excellent woman of Proverbs 31?

   _____

   _____

   What evidences do you find throughout Proverbs 31:10-31 of her...

   ...financial strength?

   ...domestic strength?

   ...physical strength?

   ...spiritual strength?

...mental strength?

Look up the words *strength* and *dignity* in a dictionary. Then write a definition of each in your own words.

—strength

—dignity

2. *Her clothing for the future*—What does verse 25 say about this godly woman's attitude toward the future?

Several other translations read "she smiles at the future" and "she laughs at the time to come."[29] I like what author Anne Ortlund shares about this woman's ability to smile and laugh at her future—it "puts the lines on her face in the right places."[30]

Developing Godly Excellence...

• *Your clothing of godly character*—We've been faithfully making our way through the treasures that make up the character of the godly woman of Proverbs 31. So far, we've covered verses 10-24. That's 15 verses! Her list of godly character is definitely growing...and we've not even finished! But this is a good time for us to review. How is *your* list looking? Share three of the virtues we've studied that have impacted your daily life. Then spend time thanking God for His model and for His movement in your life.

1.

2.

3.

- *Your clothing for the future*—As you look ahead through the corridor of time, what do you sense? Fear, worry, and anxiety? Or joy, peace, and eager anticipation? Take a minute to explain your answer. Then share how the truths taught in the verses that follow can better clothe you for the future.

—Psalm 23:1

—Psalm 37:3

—Psalm 37:5

—Proverbs 3:5

—Proverbs 3:26

—Philippians 4:19

A Heart in Pursuit of Excellence

How wonderful to wake up each and every day confident in the Lord and in the future He has for you. And how wonderful to spend each day doing our part so that we can be confident that we have indeed prepared. Then truly, the results—and the future—are in God's hands!

Being able to confidently rejoice in the future requires clothing yourself today with the garment of strength and the ornament of dignity. So here are a few "just for today" thoughts.

*J*ust for today…give your life afresh to God and proceed full-faith ahead into your beautiful day. Just for today…wholeheartedly pour out your love and care for your family and be "too nice"! Just for today…think about your positive contributions to the family finances. Just for today…take your physical "strength" seriously and exert yourself. Just for today…eliminate the misuse of your mind and instead use that brain power God has given you to grow more beautiful in character. Just for today…reach out and encourage your best friend in her spiritual journey….Finally, just for today…make the commitment to wake up every day of your life and repeat this pattern for beauty. Then you, too, can stand fully robed in your virtues, look down the corridor of time toward your unknown future, and rejoice![31]

Lesson 19

A Godly Woman Is...Wise

h, my! Prepare yourself for a most practical—and diffi-cult—lesson in godly living! As we learned in our first lesson, one of the simple teaching tools of this poetic passage is *synthetic parallelism*. That means in a simple two-line verse, the thought of the first line is continued in the second line, starting with the tiny word "and." And, my dear friend, that's what we have here. And is it ever a good one! Why? Because it has to do with our mouth and our speech. Oh, my!

Discovering the Treasure....

Begin by reading Proverbs 31:10-31 in your personal Bible. Check here when done _____. Then write out verse 26.

1. *Her mouth*—In Proverbs 31:20 we noticed the open hands (and heart) of this godly woman. And now what do we see "open" up?

Once open, what do we witness?

Think about it—This dear woman runs a household. She has a husband to converse with (verses 11,12, and 23). She has children to instruct (verse 28). She has helpers she must communicate with (verse 15). She converses with the poor and needy (verse 20). Plus she shops, bargains, and barters with a multitude of merchants (verses 13,14,16, and 24). That's a lot of people to interact with verbally! And here, in this one line, we learn that the aim of her words in her verbal exchanges with the people in her life is to do so with *wisdom.*

What do these scriptures teach us about the mouth?

—Proverbs 10:11

—Proverbs 10:14

—Proverbs 10:31

—Proverbs 11:13

—Proverbs 17:28

2. *Her words*—We now know that God's treasured woman opens her mouth with wisdom. Now what else do we learn about her words from verse 26?

What do these scriptures teach us about our words?

—Proverbs 4:24

—Proverbs 10:19

—Proverbs 12:18

—Proverbs 15:1

—Proverbs 15:23

—Proverbs 16:21

—Proverbs 16:23-24

Now let's add a few New Testament principles for the words we speak. What do we learn in...

...Ephesians 4:25?

...Ephesians 4:29?

...Ephesians 4:31-32?

...1 Timothy 3:11?

...Titus 2:3?

...Titus 3:2?

Developing Godly Excellence...

- *Your mouth*—As you look back over your discoveries about what the Bible says about a godly mouth, what three new principles for *your mouth* can you formulate and purpose to put into practice?

    1.

2.

3.

- *Your words*—As you look back over your discoveries about what the Bible says about the words of a godly woman, what three new principles for *your words* can you formulate and purpose to put into practice?

  1.

  2.

  3.

- *The mouths and words of others*—I can think right now of some other women in the Bible who show us several good formulas for our speech so that we, too, may open our mouths with wisdom and speak with kindness. What do you learn from these wise and godly women? What happened when they opened their mouths?

  —Mary in Luke 1:46-47

  —Anna in Luke 2:38

—The older women in Titus 2:3-4

* *Your heart*—As we close, what did Jesus say about the relationship between your mouth and your heart in Luke 6:45?

What advice does Solomon have for your heart in Proverbs 4:23?

A Heart in Pursuit of Excellence

Have you ever thought about what you might want engraved on your tombstone as a lasting tribute to your life? Well, if you ever do give it some thought, Proverbs 31:26 would be a most noble and excellent tribute…if it were lived out in you. So why not pursue such godly excellence in speech now? Today? And every day? Why not have it be said of you today that…

She opens her mouth with wisdom,
And on her tongue is the law of kindness.

Lesson 20

A Godly Woman Is...Prudent

y son-in-law Paul is a Navy submariner, and on several occasions Jim and I have been allowed to tour his boat (submarines are boats, not ships). The apparent size of these boats is very deceptive. They don't look very big as you observe them in the water. But once exposed in drydock, they appear massive...and they are—almost the length of two football fields and the height of a four-story building! As an officer, Paul is often the officer on duty, which means he is responsible for billions of dollars of equipment during his watch.

Well, dear watchful sister, your little place called home is worth even more than a United States nuclear submarine to your family. And you—yes, you!—are the "officer on duty" day in, day out.

How can we adequately handle such a responsibility? As always, the excellent Proverbs 31 woman shows us how.

Discovering the Treasure...

Begin by reading Proverbs 31:10-31 in your personal Bible. Check here when done _____. Then write out verse 27.

1. *Her household*—As you observe this woman from Proverbs 31, what do you now find her doing in verse 27 when it comes to the place and the people that make up her home?

   Looking back at these verses from Proverbs 31, how do you see her stewardship of her household lived out in...

   ...verse 14?

   ...verse 15?

   ...verse 21?

I call such management *prudent*. Look this word up in your dictionary and write out a brief, memorable definition of the word *prudent*.

2. *Her self*—As you further observe this godly woman's prudent activities at home, what fundamental principle guides her daily life?

Looking back at these verses from Proverbs 31, how do you see her living out this principle for her personal life in...

...verse 13?

...verse 15?

...verse 16?

...verse 18?

...verse 19?

...verses 22 and 24?

Developing Godly Excellence...

- *Your household*—There's no doubt about it: Married or single, godly excellence can be lived out at home and in our home management. We've already looked at these scriptures, but once again, what do they teach us?

—Proverbs 9:1-2

—Proverbs 14:1

—Proverbs 24:3-4

The word *ways* means the general comings and goings, the habits and orderly activities of the people at home. As you observe the ways of your household and the habits and activities of the people who come and go and who live there, what have you noticed? Is there anything you need to remedy? Are there any alarms going off? Or is all in order, is all well? (If this is true, be sure to thank God!) What will you do about anything you notice that is disturbing? Draw up a "battle plan" now.

• *Your self*—Not only does this prudent woman watch over her household, but she watches over herself, too! And so must you and I. Again, what fundamental principle guides her daily personal life?

And what do these proverbs teach about eating the bread of idleness and its results?

—Proverbs 6:9-11

—Proverbs 10:4-5

—Proverbs 12:24

—Proverbs 19:15

—Proverbs 20:4

—Proverbs 26:14

Proverbs 31:27 is a two-part description, half spoken in the positive and half in the negative. In the exercise above, you planned some specific steps in your battle plan that you will take toward strengthening the positive. Now do the same to avoid the negative. As you observe the ways of yourself and your habits and activities as you go through your days, what have you noticed? Is there anything you need to remedy? Are there any alarms going off? What will you do about anything you notice that is disturbing? Draw up a "battle plan" now.

A Heart in Pursuit of Excellence

Well, my dear watchful sister, just like my son-in-law and his submarine, you, too, have something to watch over. You are placed in your home by God as "officer on duty." And just like that submarine that doesn't appear to be very impressive with so much of it hidden from view underwater, so your home, which on the surface doesn't seem to be "a big deal," is in reality a great and privileged responsibility. When you think about it, your home and its contents make up a considerable amount of your family's assets. And no price tag can be put on the souls of your precious ones and the nurturing atmosphere of your home. Surely these treasures are worth your prudent watchcare! Therefore you must be careful as "officer on duty" to guard what has been entrusted to you. You must pursue excellence in these two vital areas of your life—the care of your household and the care of yourself. May it be said of you and me, she was a prudent manager of her household...and of herself!

Lesson 21

A Godly Woman Is...Loving

eing a wife and mother is a thankless job." That's what detractors say who advocate that women go elsewhere to get their strokes.

As a woman I have to admit that at times it seems like no one appreciates our hard work (Proverbs 31:27), thrift (verse 16), creativity (verse 22), and our positive outlook on life (verse 25). Many a wife and mother can go for days without a single "thank you" from those she serves, whether at home, at church, or at work. This might be hard for a woman to take unless she remembers that she isn't serving man but is instead serving the Lord (Colossians 3:23-24). But it's also true that on that rare occasion when someone says "thank you" out of the blue or compliments you on your efforts, it many times

117

makes all your hard work seem worth it. Do you imagine that on occasion even the Proverbs 31 woman felt that way when those close to her looked up, realized how lucky they were, and rendered a "thank you"? Hmmm....

Discovering the Treasure....

Begin by reading Proverbs 31:10-31 in your personal Bible. Check here when done _____. Then write out verse 28.

1. *Her children*—This is our first and only glimpse of the children of the Proverbs 31 woman. What do we find them doing in Proverbs 31:28?

For your information, the "rising up," however it was done, whether literally rising up and standing up or figuratively growing up and going on to live in a way that honored her, these children are paying tribute to their beloved mother.

2. *Her husband*—What other voice of tribute is heard in verse 28?

And what is he doing?

Look ahead to verse 29. What are his actual words of praise?

Developing Godly Excellence...

- *Your children*—As I shared above, if you have children, you can sometimes go a long time without a "Thank you, Mom!" But as mothers we should be much more concerned about the quality of our lives and our love for our children than we are about receiving praise. What are some of the roles we must fulfill as mothers according to...

  ...Proverbs 31, verse 15?

  ...verse 21?

  ...verse 22?

  ...verse 26?

  ...verse 27?

  ...verse 30?

  ...Proverbs 22:6?

  ...Titus 2:4?

Beloved, if we major on and fulfill these roles, we shall receive our Lord's "Well done, good and faithful servant" (and mom!)! Are there any areas where you are falling short on God's assignment to you as a mother? Pick one and write out here exactly what you plan to do about it. Sometimes a problem defined is a problem half solved!

- *Your husband*—As a wife you can, unfortunately, also go a long time without a "Thank you, dear!" But as wives we should also be much more concerned about the quality of our life and loving our husband than we are about receiving praise. What are some of the roles we must fulfill as wives according to…

  …Proverbs 31, verse 11?

  …verse 12?

  …verse 23?

  …verse 25?

  …Ephesians 5:22?

  …Ephesians 5:33?

  …Titus 2:4?

Again, if we major on and fulfill these roles, we shall receive our Lord's "Well done, good and faithful servant" (and wife)! Are there any areas where you are falling short on God's assignment to you as a wife? Pick one and write out here exactly what you plan to do about it.

A Heart in Pursuit of Excellence

As we let the seriousness of our roles and assignments from God to us as mothers and wives sink in, I have a favorite story to share with you about a very ordinary woman who took her role of motherhood seriously. I found it so moving that I wept as I read it. This, my dear, dear friend, is exactly what I want for myself and for you!

The Mother of Bill Bright

The mother of Bill Bright, founder of Campus Crusade for Christ, was described as an "ordinary" woman. Yet as she lay dying at age 93, 109 members of her family, including children, grandchildren, great-grandchildren and great-great-grandchildren, made their way to her bedside to express their love and appreciation. All of them wanted to rise up and call her "blessed."[32]

esson 22

A Godly Woman Is...Excellent

his may sound like a "poor me" testimony, but I have never been first in anything. I've never won a baking contest or any other kind of contest. I've never won a race. I never played first-chair violin in my junior high school orchestra. I didn't graduate first in my class in high school. I have to say I've always been average. And you know what? That's OK. Why? Because God says that I am "fearfully and wonderfully made" just the way I am (Psalm 139:14).

But there is one area and arena where I can be the best—be first—and that's in my home. As I expend my energies and my love on that little place called home, it becomes a refuge and a solace for those who come under its roof. Do you want to be a woman of excellence (and I know you do!)? Then do this one thing—excel at home! That's what the Proverbs 31 woman did...and did excellently.

Discovering the Treasure...

Begin by reading Proverbs 31:10-31 in your personal Bible. Check here when done _____. Then write out verse 29.

1. *Her praise*—What did the Proverbs 31 woman's fortu-nate—and grateful—husband say in verse 29 of...

   ...the many?

   ...his wife?

2. *Her excellence*—Do you remember the story about the man in the museum (see page 21) who looked long and hard at one painting? Well, dear one, realize that Proverbs 31:10-31 is God's portrait of the ideal woman. Therefore I'm about to repeat myself in your exercise. But keep in mind that I want you to *know* this woman, to *really* know her, to know all about her, about her schedule, her lifestyle, her home, her family, her hobbies and pursuits, her character qualities, her values—her heart. I want you to write her virtues "on the tablet of your heart" (Proverbs 3:3). I want you to know her well enough to point others to her and explain her excellence to them.

And now for your exercise—look again at this truly amazing woman. Scan each verse and, in a word or two, pinpoint the traits that made her so excellent.

—verse 10   —verse 20

—verse 11   —verse 21

—verse 12   —verse 22

—verse 13   —verse 23

—verse 14   —verse 24

—verse 15   —verse 25

—verse 16   —verse 26

—verse 17   —verse 27

—verse 18   —verse 30

—verse 19   —verse 31

That's quite a portrait, isn't it? A true masterpiece!

Developing Godly Excellence...

• *Your praise*—Choose three of this godly woman's excellent traits from above that you believe made her husband able to say that she excelled above all the other excellent women. Write them here. Then make a brief to-do list for yourself so that you, too, can—by God's grace—excel even more in these areas. And remember, whether you are married or single, you can pursue and seek after almost every one of these godly qualities.

1.

2.

3.

- *Your husband*—Just a note...if you are married, don't forget to praise your husband! Don't have him go for days on end without hearing your "Thank you, honey!" No excellent wife would fail to praise her husband! Now, what praise will you express today?

A Heart in Pursuit of Excellence

It would be lovely indeed to have someone—anyone!—say the words to and of you that this noble wife's husband uttered! His chorus of praise resounds as he declares: "You surpass them all! You transcend them all! You far outdo them all! You are better than all of them!"[33] In other words, he points out that other women "do" their activities (and do them with excellence), but he praises his wife because of her very character—she "is" excellent![34]

As the saying goes, "Character counts!" And, I might add, it counts *mightily* when it comes to excellence.

esson 23

A Godly Woman Is...Reverent

Proverbs 31:30

Mirror, mirror, on the wall,
Who's the fairest of them all?

his is a fairy-tale question every woman is familiar with. And, hopefully, after 22 lessons in this study of the many treasures of the godly woman of Proverbs 31, both you and I know the answer! Truly, *she* is the fairest of them all! And how about you and me? While it may be true that once upon a time we were some of the "fair" ones, we must admit today that our outward beauty is on the decline. Like all temporal things, it was...and then is no more.

But true beauty—hidden beauty, inner beauty, lasting beauty, the beauty of the heart spoken of in 1 Peter 3:3-4— can be ours as we focus our lives on the spiritual life instead of physical beauty. Read now, as, in an almost parenthetical way, the writer of Proverbs 31:10-31 steps back from the physical accomplishments of this remarkable lady and states that ultimate praise comes for a woman who is reverent of soul, a woman who fears the Lord.

Discovering the Treasure...

Begin by reading Proverbs 31:10-31 in your personal Bible. Check here when done _____. Then write out verse 30.

1. *Twin vanities*—If, as we noted at the beginning of our study, a godly mother is indeed teaching her young son (Proverbs 31:1-2) this bit of alphabetical wisdom about what kind of woman to marry (Proverbs 31:10-31), I like to imagine her hitting the ceiling on this verse and letter of the alphabet. Now, I know she wouldn't do that (see verses 25 and 26!), but I'm sure she was dead serious when she got to this core quality of a reverence for God in a woman's heart. What two vanities in a woman does she warn her young charge against, and how does she describe them?

Look up the word *charm* in a dictionary and write out a definition.

Also look up the word *beauty* in a dictionary and write out a definition.

2. *A reverent spirit*—Instead, what virtue—and what kind of woman—is held up as truly praiseworthy?

Look up the word *reverent* in a dictionary and write out a definition.

Developing Godly Excellence...

- *Charm is deceitful*—Charm is fickle and fleeting. And in the end, charm is one of life's illusions, one of life's vanities. It can never produce happiness or get the work of life done. What misuse of charm is described in the following proverbs?

—Proverbs 5:3

—Proverbs 7:21

—Proverbs 21:6

- *Beauty is vain*—Beauty is only skin deep, and it, too, is fleeting as it fades. Beauty does not guarantee a happy life, nor does it effectively manage the nuts-and-bolts realities of life. What is our only hope for beauty according to...

  ...Proverbs 31:30?

  ...2 Corinthians 4:16?

  ...1 Timothy 2:9-10?

  ...Titus 2:3?

  ...1 Peter 3:3-4?

- *The beauty of the Lord*—In stark contrast to the temporary and fleeting vanities of charm and good looks is the everlasting beauty of "the fear of the Lord." What insights do these proverbs give about "the fear of the Lord"?

  —Proverbs 1:7

  —Proverbs 8:13

—Proverbs 9:10

—Proverbs 15:33

—Proverbs 22:4

According to Proverbs 31:30, it is better for a woman to fear the Lord than to have _____ and _____, and a woman who fears the Lord shall be _____.

A Heart in Pursuit of Excellence

I'm assuming that yours, dear one, is a heart in pursuit of excellence if you have stayed with this study to this point, to Lesson 23! But a love and reverence for the Lord begins with a relationship with Jesus Christ. In case you're not sure about how to have a relationship with Jesus Christ, let me invite you to establish one today and so begin living a life of true internal, eternal beauty! You can set foot on the path of growing in godly beauty right now by earnestly praying words like these from your heart:

> Jesus, I know I am a sinner, but I want to repent of my sins and turn to follow You. I believe that

You died for my sins and rose again victorious over the power of sin and death, and I want to accept You as my personal Savior. Come into my life, Lord Jesus, and help me obey You from this day forward.

I'm praying for you right now! True and lasting beauty—indeed, all beauty—begins in Jesus Christ!

Lesson 24

A Godly Woman Is...Virtuous

omeone has well said, "Our lives are made up of a single day repeated. What you are tomorrow, you are becoming today." My friend, our treasured Proverbs 31 woman didn't become who she was overnight. What we are seeing in this wonderful lady is the disciplined life of godly behavior repeated, day after day, that in time emerged as a life of magnificence.

Dear one, every day you and I have a choice about how we will spend that day, that one precious, priceless day. If we choose to build on the shifting sands of undisciplined living, we will one day wake up to see the tide wash away our little sandcastle. I urge you, as we bring our study to a close, to determine, with God's help, to choose to build your life on the solid bedrock of God-honoring disciplines that will withstand the crashing waves of time and trials. When the storms of life subside and the waves calm, then, by God's grace, there will stand a life—your life—for all to see and praise.

Discovering the Treasure...

Begin by reading Proverbs 31:10-31 in your personal Bible. Check here when done _____. Then write out verse 31.

1. *Her hands*—What is the first thing the reader (and everyone else) is instructed to do regarding the Proverbs 31 woman?

Look once again at these descriptions of this godly woman's hands. What do you recall from these verses in Proverbs 31?

—Verse 13

—Verse 19

—Verse 20

—Verse 31

How many different character qualities and God-honoring disciplines do you see lived out in these verses?

2. *Her praise*—What has this worthy woman's works reaped for her?

Developing Godly Excellence...

- *Your hands*—What message do the following proverbs offer your heart—and your hands—about the beauty and value of hard work and a life of discipline? (Prepare yourself for some repeats here, but I believe we cannot handle these basics of excellence often enough!)

  —Proverbs 14:23

  —Proverbs 27:18

  —Proverbs 28:19

  —Proverbs 31:13

  —Proverbs 31:31

- *Your praise*—We know that the contributions that the Proverbs 31 woman made to her husband, her children, her household, and her community are most praiseworthy. But what about your praise? Here are two questions for you to ponder.

—What does Proverbs 27:2 say you are to do—or not do?

—What does Proverbs 31:30 say merits praise? (And therefore, what are *you* to do?)

• *In praise of the Proverbs 31 woman*—What a wonderful harvest of praise we witness on behalf of this godly woman as our study comes to a true crescendo-like ending! Who do you notice praising her in...

...verse 28?

...verses 28-29?

...verse 30?

...verse 31?

Now, for what do you praise her most, and why? Add your voice to this chorus of praise!

A Heart in Pursuit of Excellence

I'm sure you're a woman who prays regularly about God's will for your life. After all, that's what a woman after God's own heart is—a woman who will fulfill all *God's* will (Acts 13:22).

Well, beloved seeker of His will, I hope by now that you have a better understanding about God's will for your life. Indeed, the godly woman of Proverbs 31 has been our tutor as well as our model of exactly what God's will is for us!

And now for...

A Fitting Conclusion

This verse forms a fitting conclusion to what is the most remarkable exposition in the Old Testament on the position of women, exalting... her functions in the home as wife, mother, and mistress, and showing how contentedness and happiness in the domestic circle depend upon the foresight and oversight of this queen of the hearth.[35]

Lesson 25

A Godly Woman Is…a Treasure!

*E*veryone loves a parade! And definitely one of the benefits of living in Southern California for so many years was the annual opportunity to personally view up close the breathtaking floats after the world-famous Rose Parade. After the one million-plus people who had lined the streets of Pasadena to watch the parade go home, the expensive and impressive floats are parked away from the city on view for those who want to take a closer look, to marvel at their amazing artistry, and to inspect the variety of ingredients (every component is required to be a part of a plant) used to create such exquisite beauty.

Well, dear one, our parade is over. We've now watched the 22 character qualities that make up the heart and soul of the godly woman of Proverbs 31 file by. I admit, it was a lot to take in. But now, as we stand together at the end of our exhilarating journey of discovering the treasures that make her God's ideal woman, we have a final opportunity to inspect them one by one. Let's do it now.

Reviewing the treasure...

Begin by reading Proverbs 31:10-31 one final time in your personal Bible. Check here when done _____.

God's treasured woman—She's incredible, isn't she? She's a biblical treasure! And remember again that she teaches us God's alphabet of godly virtues. Whenever I teach Proverbs 31:10-31, I actually teach it as an alphabet. I've assigned a word to each of the 22 verses that describes or defines the character quality portrayed there. And now I want you to try your hand at just such an exercise. I've listed the alphabetical letters below. As you look again at each verse, assign it a short title. And have fun...just like the writer did as he penned these ABCs of God's ideal woman! (And, just to get you started, I've included my first three titles as examples. List your own titles and continue on.)

Verse 10—A   Army

Verse 11—B   Blessing

Verse 12—C   Considerate

Verse 13—D

Verse 14—E

Verse 15—F

Verse 16—G

Verse 17—H

Verse 18—I

Verse 19—J

Verse 20—K

Verse 21—L

Verse 22—M

Verse 23—N

Verse 24—O

Verse 25—P

Verse 26—Q

Verse 27—R

Verse 28—S

Verse 29—T

Verse 30—U

Verse 31—V

Becoming...
A woman after God's own heart...

Precious new friend and sister-in-Christ, our journey is minutes away from being over. The sun is setting on our time together. But just think about it...that same sun is rising on all your tomorrows as God's Word has now given you a better, richer, and deeper understanding and appreciation for the Proverbs 31 woman and how God desires you and me to live each day. He has revealed His standard and shown us a model who was most definitely a woman after God's own heart.

Now the question is, how can you and I continue becoming women after God's own heart too, women who desire to fulfill all God's will (Acts 13:22)? How can we continue to follow in the steps of the terrific woman God sets before us?

I think a fitting ending exercise is this—

1. Pray and thank God for Proverbs 31 and for giving you an example of feminine excellence.

2. Pray through your alphabetical list. Acknowledge the Proverbs 31 woman's character and accomplishments. Acknowledge that her excellence is God's ideal for you, too.

3. Pray and thank God for the areas where you've seen growth during your study and where you sense that, with

His able assistance, you have some kind of handle on the virtues.

4. Star or circle areas that need improvement. Once again, map out a "battle plan." Ask God for His help, and then move out on your plan. That, dear one, is how you (and I!) continue to become a woman after God's own heart!

May our Lord richly bless you as you continue to grow into the godly woman He desires you to be, with...

a heart in pursuit of excellence

Leading a Bible Study Discussion Group

What a privilege it is to lead a Bible study! And what joy and excitement await you as you delve into the Word of God and help others to discover its life-changing truths. If God has called you to lead a Bible study group, I know you'll be spending much time in prayer and planning and giving much thought to being an effective leader. I also know that taking the time to read through the following tips will help you to navigate the challenges of leading a Bible study discussion group and enjoying the effort and opportunity.

The Leader's Roles

As a Bible study group leader, you'll find your role changing back and forth from *expert* to *cheerleader* to *lover* to *referee* during the course of a session.

Since you're the leader, group members will look to you to be the *expert* guiding them through the material. So be well prepared. In fact, be over-prepared so that you know the material better than any group member does. Start your study early in the week and let its message simmer all week long. (You might even work several lessons ahead so that you have in mind the big picture and the overall direction of the study.) Be ready to share some additional gems that your group members wouldn't have discovered on their own. That extra insight from your study time—or that comment from a wise Bible teacher or scholar, that clever saying, that keen observation from another believer, and even an appropriate joke—adds an element of fun and keeps Bible study from becoming routine, monotonous, and dry.

Second, be ready to be the group's *cheerleader*. Your energy and enthusiasm for the task at hand can be contagious. It can also stimulate people to get more involved in their personal study as well as in the group discussion.

Third, be the *lover*, the one who shows a genuine concern for the members of the group. You're the one who will establish the atmosphere of the group. If you laugh and have fun, the group members will laugh and have fun. If you hug, they will hug. If you care, they will care. If you share, they will share. If you love, they will love. So pray every day to love the women God has placed in your group. Ask Him to show you how to love them with His love.

Finally, as the leader, you'll need to be the *referee* on occasion. That means making sure everyone has an equal opportunity to speak. That's easier to do when you operate under the assumption that every member of the group has something worthwhile to contribute. So, trusting that the Lord has taught each person during the week, act on that assumption.

Expert, cheerleader, lover, and referee—these four roles of the leader may make the task seem overwhelming. But that's not bad if it keeps you on your knees praying for your group.

A Good Start

Beginning on time, greeting people warmly, and opening in prayer gets the study off to a good start. Know what you want to have happen during your time together and make sure those things get done. That kind of order means comfort for those involved.

Establish a format and let the group members know what that format is. People appreciate being in a Bible study that focuses on the Bible. So keep the discussion on the topic and move the group through the questions. Tangents are often hard to avoid—and even harder to rein in. So be sure to focus on the answers to questions about the specific passage at hand. After all, the purpose of the group is Bible study!

Finally, as someone has accurately observed, "Personal growth is one of the by-products of any effective small group. This growth is achieved when people are recognized and accepted by others. The more friendliness, mutual trust, respect, and warmth exhibited, the more likely that the member will find pleasure in the group, and, too, the more likely she will work hard toward the accomplishment of the group's goals. The effective leader will strive to reinforce desirable traits" (source unknown).

A Dozen Helpful Tips

Here is a list of helpful suggestions for leading a Bible study discussion group:

1. Arrive early, ready to focus fully on others and give of yourself. If you have to do any last-minute preparation, review, re-grouping, or praying, do it in the car. Don't dash in, breathless, harried, late, still tweaking your plans.

2. Check out your meeting place in advance. Do you have everything you need—tables, enough chairs, a blackboard, hymnals if you plan to sing, coffee, etc.?

3. Greet each person warmly by name as she arrives. After all, you've been praying for these women all week long, so let each VIP know that you're glad she's arrived.

4. Use name tags for at least the first two or three weeks.

5. Start on time no matter what—even if only one person is there!

6. Develop a pleasant but firm opening statement. You might say, "This lesson was great! Let's get started so we

can enjoy all of it!" or "Let's pray before we begin our lesson."

7. Read the questions, but don't hesitate to reword them on occasion. Rather than reading an entire paragraph of instructions, for instance, you might say, "Question 1 asks us to list some ways that Christ displayed humility. Lisa, please share one way Christ displayed humility."

8. Summarize or paraphrase the answers given. Doing so will keep the discussion focused on the topic, eliminate digressions, help avoid or clear up any misunderstandings of the text, and keep each group member aware of what the others are saying.

9. Keep moving and don't add any of your own questions to the discussion time. It's important to get through the study guide questions. So if a cut-and-dried answer is called for, you don't need to comment with anything other than a "thank you." But when the question asks for an opinion or an application (for instance, "How can this truth help us in our marriages?" or "How do *you* find time for your quiet time?"), let all who want to contribute.

10. Affirm each person who contributes, especially if the contribution was very personal, painful to share, or a quiet person's rare statement. Make everyone who shares a hero by saying something like "Thank you for sharing that insight from your own life" or "We certainly appreciate what God has taught you. Thank you for letting us in on it."

11. Watch your watch, put a clock right in front of you, or consider using a timer. Pace the discussion so that you meet your cut-off time, especially if you want time to pray. Stop at the designated time even if you haven't finished the lesson. Remember that everyone has worked through the study once; you are simply going over it again.

12. End on time. You can only make friends with your group members by ending on time or even a little early! Besides, members of your group have the next item on their agenda to attend to—picking up children from the nursery, babysitter, or school; heading home to tend to matters there; running errands; getting to bed; or spending some time with their husbands. So let them out *on time!*

Five Common Problems

In any group, you can anticipate certain problems. Here are some common ones that can arise, along with helpful solutions:

1. *The incomplete lesson*—Right from the start, establish the policy that if someone has not done the lesson, it is best for her not to answer the questions. But do try to include her responses to questions that ask for opinions or experiences. Everyone can share some thoughts in reply to a question like, "Reflect on what you know about both athletic and spiritual training and then share what you consider to be the essential elements of training oneself in godliness."

2. *The gossip*—The Bible clearly states that gossiping is wrong, so you don't want to allow it in your group. Set a high and strict standard by saying, "I am not comfortable with this conversation," or "We [not *you*] are gossiping, ladies. Let's move on."

3. *The talkative member*—Here are three scenarios and some possible solutions for each.

   a. The problem talker may be talking because she has done her homework and is excited about something she has to share. She may also know more about the subject than the others and, if you cut her off, the rest of the group may suffer.

SOLUTION: Respond with a comment like: "Sarah, you are making very valuable contributions. Let's see if we can get some reactions from the others," or "I know Sarah can answer this. She's really done her homework. How about some of the rest of you?"

b. The talkative member may be talking because she has *not* done her homework and wants to contribute, but she has no boundaries.

SOLUTION: Establish at the first meeting that those who have not done the lesson do not contribute except on opinion or application questions. You may need to repeat this guideline at the beginning of each session.

c. The talkative member may want to be heard whether or not she has anything worthwhile to contribute.

SOLUTION: After subtle reminders, be more direct, saying, "Betty, I know you would like to share your ideas, but let's give others a chance. I'll call on you later."

4. *The quiet member*—Here are two scenarios and possible solutions.

a. The quiet member wants the floor but somehow can't get the chance to share.

SOLUTION: Clear the path for the quiet member by first watching for clues that she wants to speak (moving to the edge of her seat, looking as if she wants to speak, perhaps even starting to say something) and then saying, "Just a second. I think Chris wants to say something." Then, of course, make her a hero!

b. The quiet member simply doesn't want the floor.

Solution: "Chris, what answer do you have on question 2?" or "Chris, what do you think about…?" Usually after a shy person has contributed a few times, she will become more confident and more ready to share. Your role is to provide an opportunity where there is *no* risk of a wrong answer. But occasionally a group member will tell you that she would rather not be called on. Honor her request, but from time to time ask her privately if she feels ready to contribute to the group discussions.

In fact, give all your group members the right to pass. During your first meeting, explain that any time a group member does not care to share an answer, she may simply say, "I pass." You'll want to repeat this policy at the beginning of every group session.

5. *The wrong answer*—Never tell a group member that she has given a wrong answer, but at the same time never let a wrong answer go by.

Solution: Either ask if someone else has a different answer or ask additional questions that will cause the right answer to emerge. As the women get closer to the right answer, say, "We're getting warmer! Keep thinking! We're almost there!"

Learning from Experience

Immediately after each Bible study session, evaluate the group discussion time using this checklist. You may also want a member of your group (or an assistant or trainee or outside observer) to evaluate you periodically.

May God strengthen—and encourage!—you as you assist others in the discovery of His many wonderful truths.

otes

1. Taken from Elizabeth George, *A Woman After God's Own Heart*® (Eugene, OR: Harvest House Publishers, 1997), pp. 24-29.

2. Robert L. Alden, *Proverbs, A Commentary on an Ancient Book of Timeless Advice* (Grand Rapids, MI: Baker Book House, 1990), p. 217.

3. Charles F. Pfeiffer and Everett F. Harrison, *The Wycliffe Bible Commentary* (Chicago, IL: Moody Press, 1973), p. 582.

4. James Strong, *Exhaustive Concordance of the Bible* (Nashville, TN: Abingdon Press, 1973), p. 39.

5. Alden, *Proverbs,* p. 220.

6. Cheryl Julia Dunn, "A Study of Proverbs 31:10-31." Master thesis, Biola University, 1993, pp. 25-26.

7. Ibid., p. 25.

8. George, *A Woman After God's Own Heart*®, p. 121.

9. Herbert Lockyer, *The Women of the Bible* (Grand Rapids, MI: Zondervan Publishing House, 1975), p. 23.

10. Albert M. Wells Jr., *Inspiring Quotations—Contemporary & Classical* (Nashville, TN: Thomas Nelson Publishers, 1988), p. 82.

11. Anonymous poem cited in John C. Maxwell and Jim Dornan, *Becoming a Person of Influence* (Nashville, TN: Thomas Nelson Publishers, 1997), p. 10.

12. William Arnot, *Studies in Proverbs—Laws from Heaven for Life on Earth* (Grand Rapids, MI: Kregel Publications, 1978), p. 575.

13. W. O. E. Oesterley, *The Book of Proverbs* (London: Methuen & Co. Ltd., 1929), p. 284.

14. Dunn, "A Study of Proverbs 31:10-31," p. 41.

15. Ibid., pp. 52-53.

16. Derek Kidner, *The Proverbs* (Downers Grove, IL: InterVarsity Press, 1973), p. 184.

17. Dunn, "A Study of Proverbs 31:10-31," p. 50.

18. Ibid., pp. 58-59.

19. Alden, *Proverbs,* p. 220.

20. Elizabeth George, *Beautiful in God's Eyes—The Treasures of the Proverbs 31 Woman* (Eugene OR: Harvest House Publishers, 1998), p. 101.

21. George, *Beautiful in God's Eyes,* p. 123.

22. Sybil Stanton, *The 25-Hour Woman* (Old Tappan, NJ: Fleming H. Revell Company, 1986), p. 169.

23. David Thomas, *Book of Proverbs Expository and Homiletical Commentary* (Grand Rapids, MI: Kregel Publications, 1982), p. 793.

24. Curtis Vaughan, ed., *The Old Testament Books of Poetry from 26 Translations* (Grand Rapids, MI: Zondervan Bible Publishers, 1973), p. 631.

25. Duane A. Garrett, *Proverbs, Ecclesiastes, Song of Solomon,* New American Commentary (Nashville, TN: Broadman Press, 1993), p. 251.

26. Dunn, "A Study of Proverbs 31:10-31," p. 101.

27. George Lawson, *Proverbs* (Grand Rapids, MI: Kregel Publications, 1980), p. 883.

28. George, *Beautiful in God's Eyes,* pp. 164-65.

29. Vaughan, *The Old Testament Books of Poetry,* p. 632.

30. Ray and Anne Ortlund, *The Best Half of Life* (Glendale, CA: Regal Books, 1976), p. 88.

31. George, *Beautiful in God's Eyes,* pp. 190-91.

32. Vonnette Zachary Bright, ed., *The Greatest Lesson I've Ever Learned* (San Bernardino, CA: Here's Life Publishers, Inc., 1991), p. 182.

33. Vaughan, *The Old Testament Books of Poetry,* pp. 632-33.

34. Dunn, "A Study of Proverbs 31:10-31," p. 163.

35. W. O. E. Oesterley, *The Book of Proverbs,* p. 283.

Personal Notes

_____

_____

_____

_____

_____

_____

_____

_____

_____

_____

_____

_____

_____

_____

_____

_____

_____

_____

_____

_____

A Woman After God's Own Heart® Study Series

Bible Studies for Busy Women

God wrote the Bible to change hearts and lives. Every study in this series is written with that in mind—and is especially focused on helping Christian women know how God desires for them to live."

—Elizabeth George

Sharing wisdom gleaned from more than 20 years as a women's Bible study teacher, Elizabeth has prepared insightful lessons that can be completed in 15 to 20 minutes per day. Each lesson includes thought-provoking questions, insights, Bible study tips, instructions for leading a discussion group, and a "heart response" section to make the Bible passage more personal.

0-7369-0816-1

Becoming a Woman of Beauty & Strength
ESTHER
Elizabeth George
0-7369-0489-1

Putting On a Gentle & Quiet Spirit
1 PETER
Elizabeth George
0-7369-0290-2

Discovering the Treasures of a Godly Woman
PROVERBS 31
Elizabeth George
0-7369-0818-8

Nurturing a Heart of Humility
CHARACTER STUDIES MARY
Elizabeth George
0-7369-0300-3

Walking in God's Promises
CHARACTER STUDIES SARAH
Elizabeth George
0-7369-0301-1

Experiencing God's Peace
PHILIPPIANS
Elizabeth George
0-7369-0289-9

Pursuing Godliness
1 TIMOTHY
Elizabeth George
0-7369-0665-7

Cultivating a Life of Character
JUDGES/RUTH
Elizabeth George
0-7369-0498-0

Growing in Wisdom & Faith
JAMES
Elizabeth George
0-7369-0490-5

HARVEST HOUSE PUBLISHERS
EUGENE, OREGON 97402
www.harvesthousepublishers.com

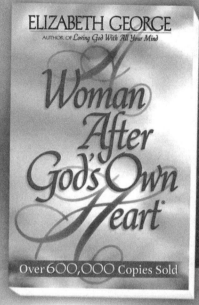

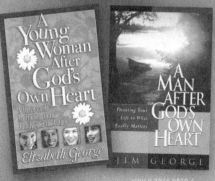

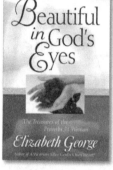

*A*bout the Author

Elizabeth George is a bestselling author and speaker whose passion is to teach the Bible in a way that changes women's lives. For information about Elizabeth's books or speaking ministry, to sign up for her mailings, or to share how God has used this book in your life, please write to Elizabeth at:

Elizabeth George
P.O. Box 2879
Belfair, WA 98528

Toll-free fax/phone: 1-800-542-4611
www.ElizabethGeorge.com

∾

Books by Elizabeth George

- Beautiful in God's Eyes
- Life Management for Busy Women
- Loving God with All Your Mind
- A Mom After God's Own Heart
- Powerful Promises for Every Woman
- The Remarkable Women of the Bible
- Small Changes for a Better Life
- A Wife After God's Own Heart
- A Woman After God's Own Heart®
- A Woman After God's Own Heart® Deluxe Edition
- A Woman's Call to Prayer
- A Woman's High Calling
- A Woman's Walk with God
- A Young Woman After God's Own Heart
- A Young Woman's Call to Prayer
- A Young Woman's Walk with God

Children's Books

- God's Wisdom for Little Girls

Study Guides

- Beautiful in God's Eyes Growth & Study Guide
- Life Management for Busy Women Growth & Study Guide
- Loving God with All Your Mind Growth & Study Guide
- A Mom After God's Own Heart Growth & Study Guide
- The Remarkable Women of the Bible Growth & Study Guide
- Small Changes for a Better Life Growth & Study Guide
- A Wife After God's Own Heart Growth & Study Guide
- A Woman After God's Own Heart® Growth & Study Guide
- A Woman's Call to Prayer Growth & Study Guide
- A Woman's High Calling Growth & Study Guide
- A Woman's Walk with God Growth & Study Guide

Books by Jim & Elizabeth George

- God Loves His Precious Children
- God's Wisdom for Little Boys

Books by Jim George

- God's Man of Influence
- A Husband After God's Own Heart
- A Man After God's Own Heart
- The Remarkable Prayers of the Bible
- The Remarkable Prayers of the Bible Growth & Study Guide
- What God Wants to Do for You
- A Young Man After God's Own Heart